A MESSAGE FOR THE BEGINNING PIANIST . . .

This unique self-teaching approach will prove to be most interesting and exciting. The remarkable results you achieve may make you decide to continue your progress with lessons from a music teacher.

Teach Yourself Piano

By Dick Bennett

Bernard Stein Music Co.

MADE IN U.S.A.

MIDDLE C
and how to find it

The Piano keyboard has 88 black and white keys. The black keys are in groups of twos and threes. C is located at the immediate left of two black keys. Middle C is above the piano pedals and below the usual location of the piano name.

the piano PEDALS

SOFT PEDAL SOSTENUTO (SUSTAIN) PEDAL DAMPER PEDAL

The pedal on the right is the damper pedal, sometimes called the "loud pedal." This pedal raises the dampers and allows the strings to vibrate until the pedal is raised. The left pedal (soft pedal) allows fewer strings to be struck by the hammers. The middle pedal raises the dampers from individual keys when they are depressed. This means a single tone can be sustained while the hand is free to play other notes.

CHORDS

1. The various chords on pages 38 through 47 are shown in their basic positions near the middle of the piano. All chords may be played one octave or two octaves higher with the right hand and one octave or two octaves lower with the left hand. The same fingering should be used when the chords are moved an octave or more.

2. Four and five note chords (7ths and 9ths) are shown with full notation and fingering, Very often one note is omitted to simplify the fingering. The omitted note, or notes, may be played with the left hand to complete the full harmony desired.

3. Augmented seventh chords are formed by raising the fifth of the dominant seventh by one half step. C, E, G, B♭, would become C, E, G♯, B♭. This chord may be indicated by C7+5 or C7♯5.

4. The fifth of the dominant seventh may be lowered by one half step. This would become C, E, G♭, B♭. This chord may be indicated by C7−5 or C7♭5.

MUSICAL NOTATION

The style of the note indicates the time value. If the Time Signature is 3/4, or 4/4, these notes would have the following values.

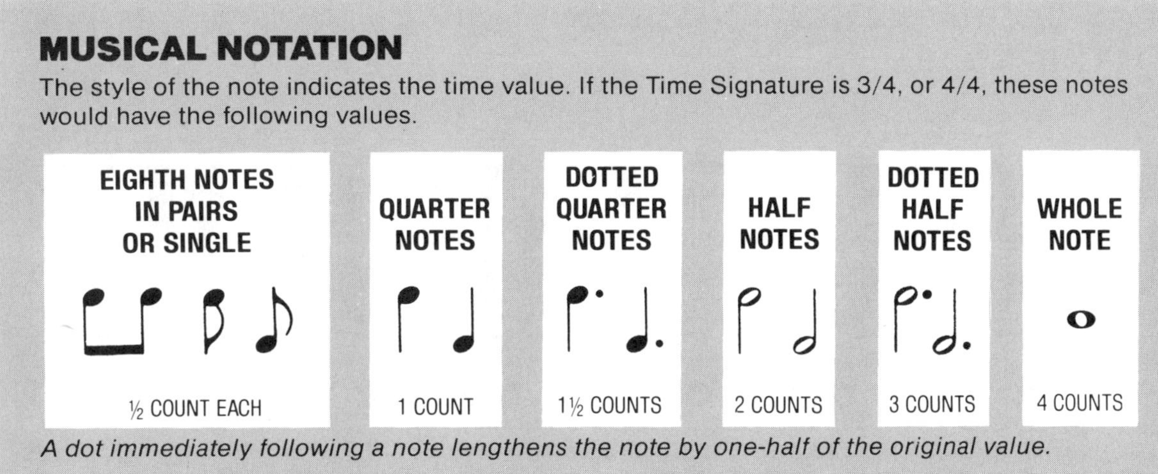

A dot immediately following a note lengthens the note by one-half of the original value.

CLEFS

THE TREBLE CLEF INDICATES MUSIC FOR THE RIGHT HAND

THE BASS CLEF INDICATES MUSIC FOR THE LEFT HAND

THE GRAND STAFF

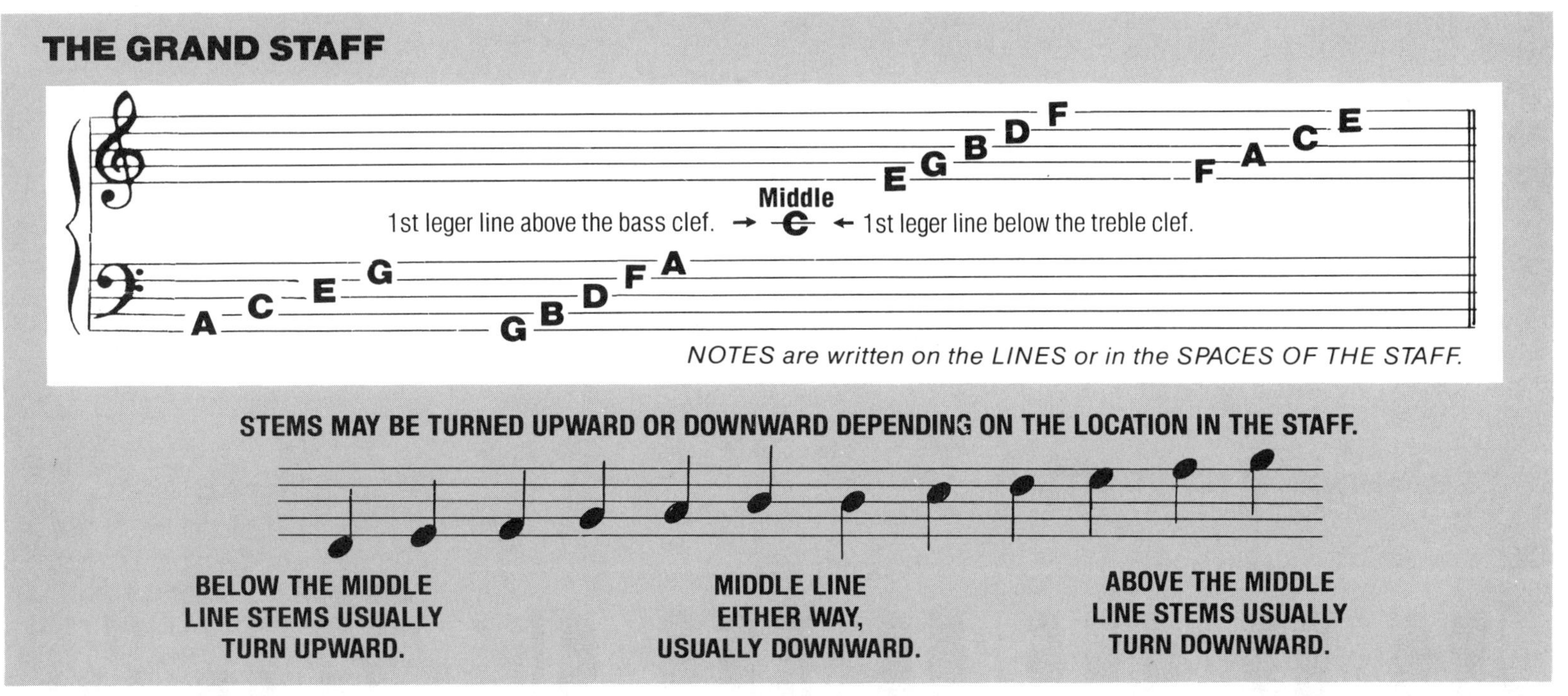

LEGER LINES

The staff can be extended by additional lines added above or below.

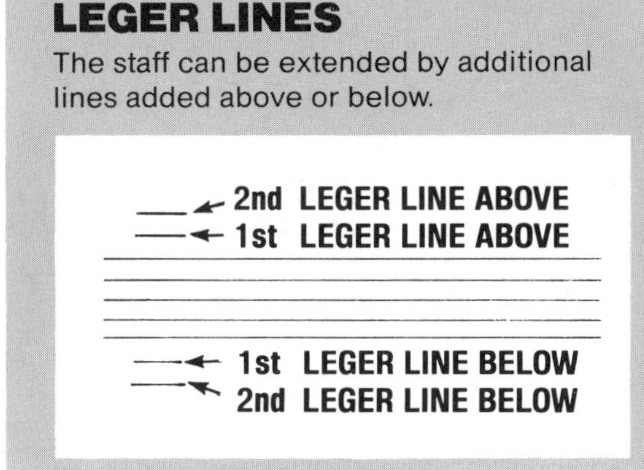

MEASURES

Music is divided into measures.
Bar lines separate each measure.

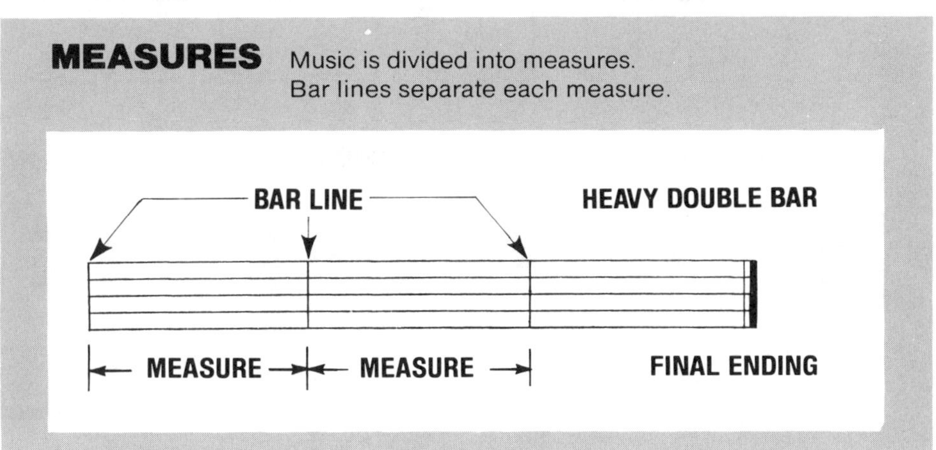

TIME SIGNATURES

THE STAFF

The staff is composed of five lines and four spaces. Lines and spaces are always counted from the bottom.

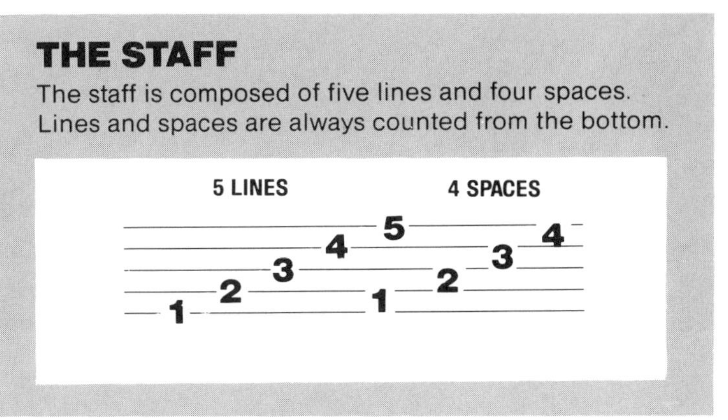

MUSICAL RANGE IN THIS BOOK

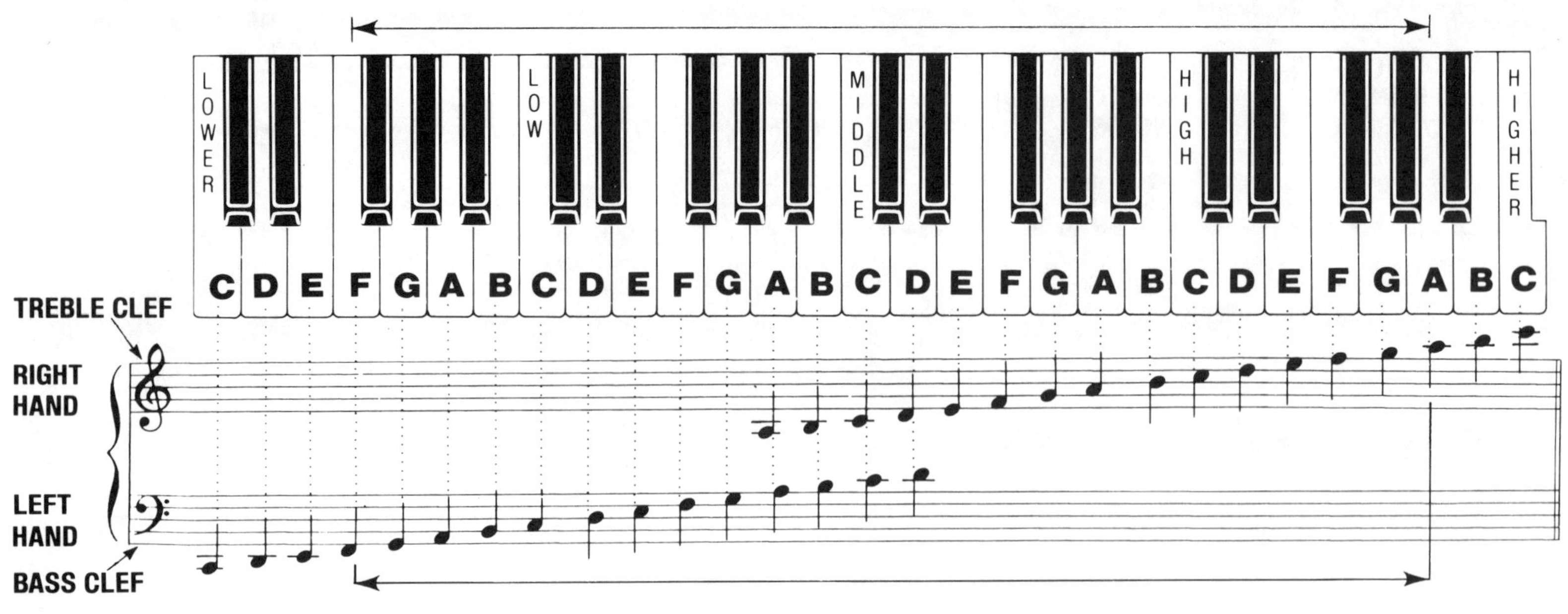

BEGINNING HAND POSITION

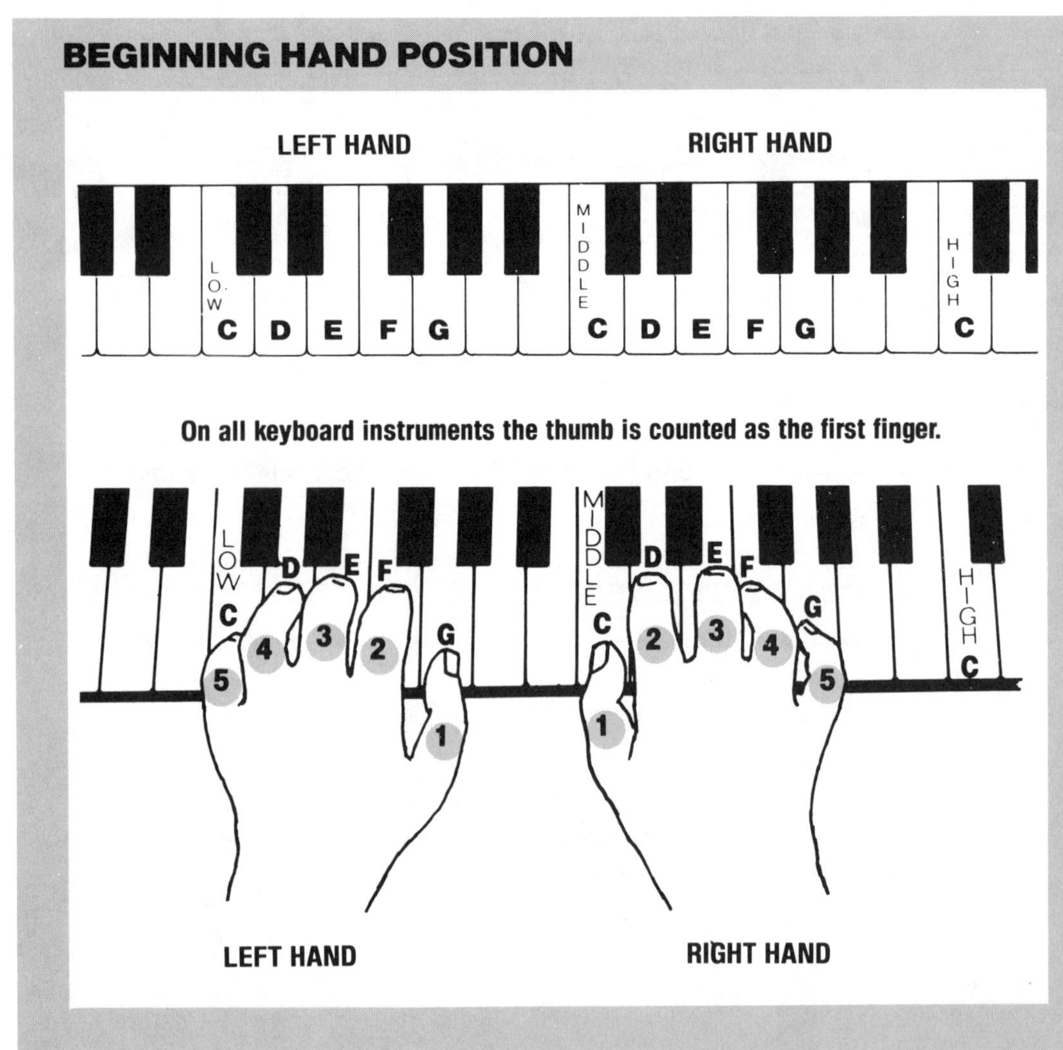

Right Hand Extension

At various times the first finger of either hand may be extended to play a key beyond the usual five finger hand position. This extension is shown by the abbreviation ext.

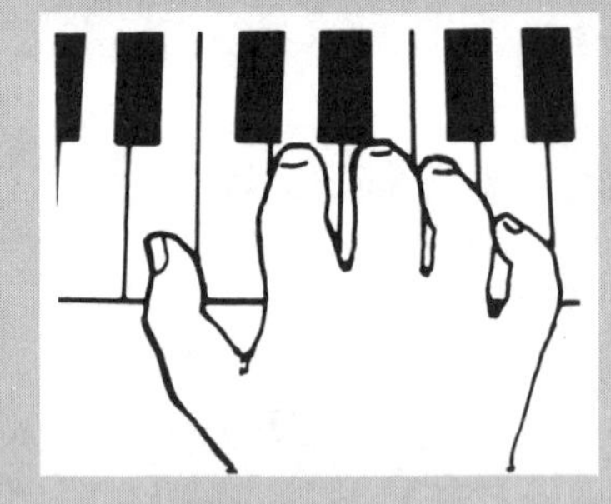

3rd Finger Crossing Over Or 1st Finger Passing Under.

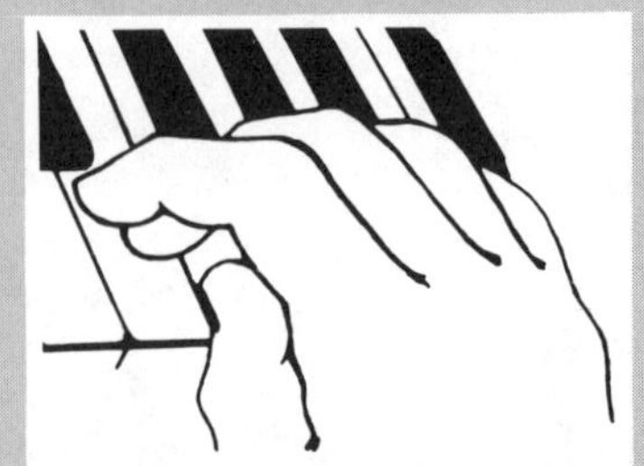

EXERCISES FOR THE RIGHT HAND

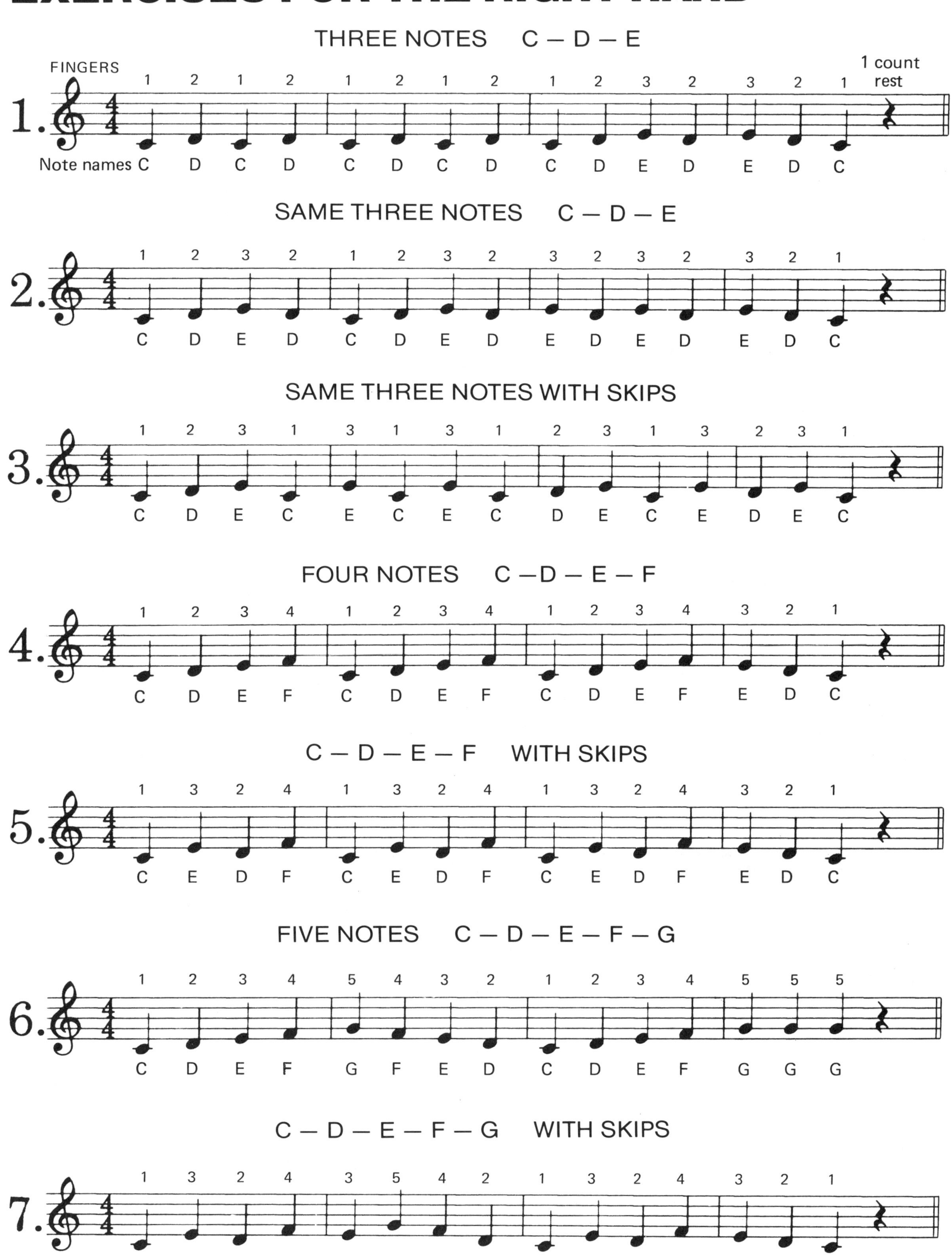

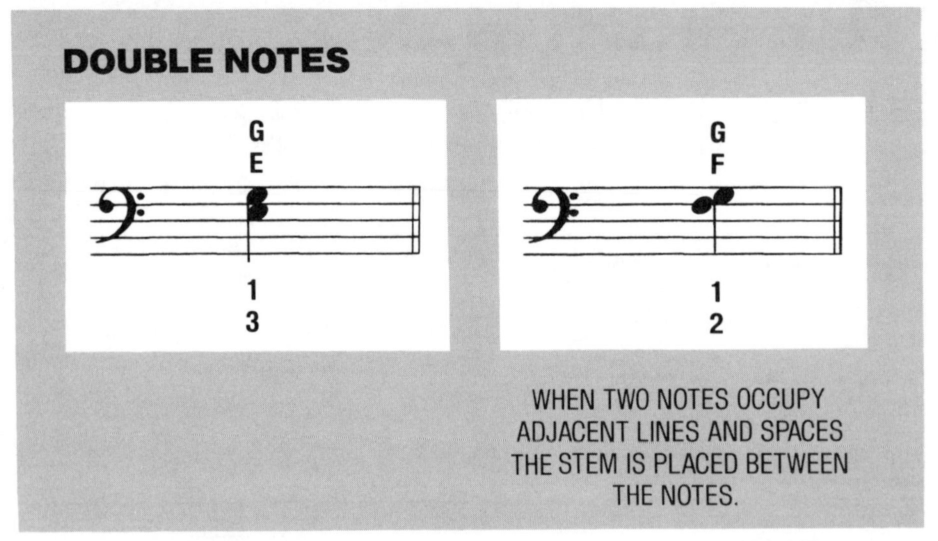

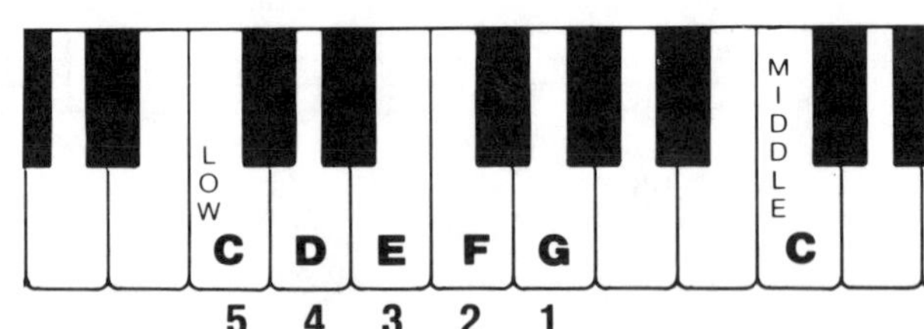

EXERCISE FOR THE LEFT HAND

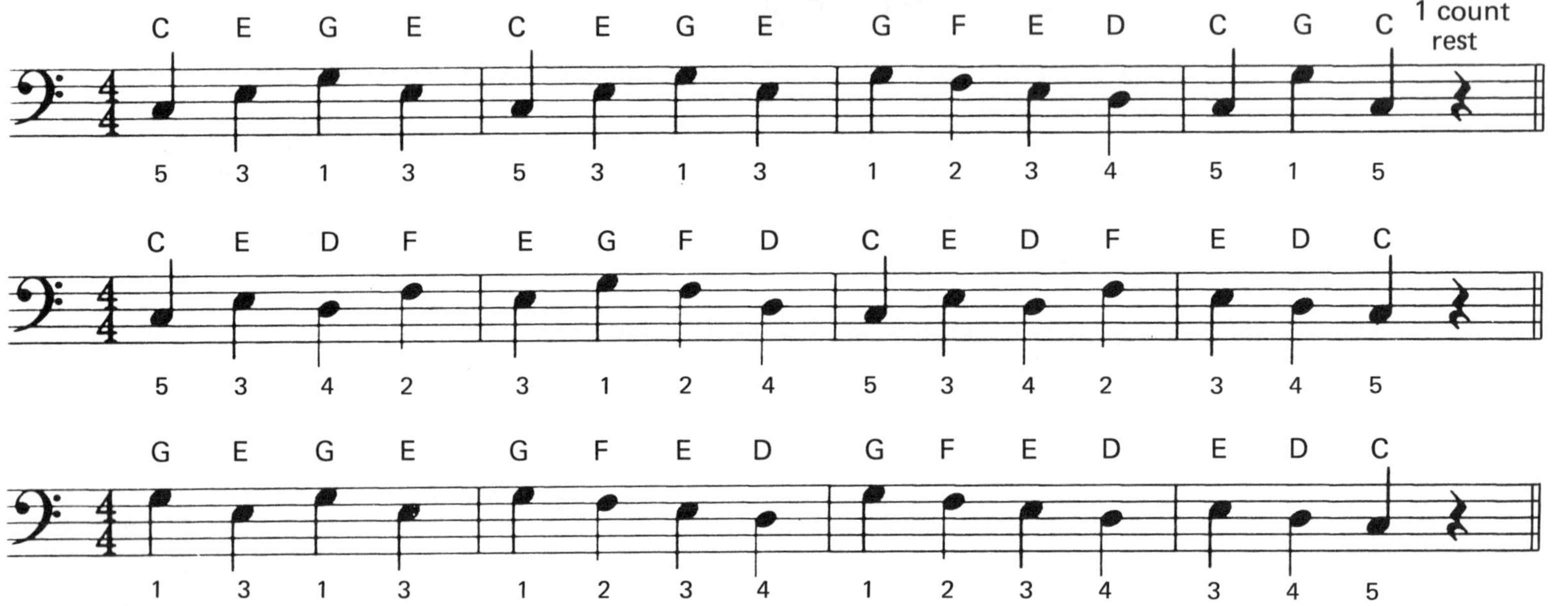

SINGLE AND DOUBLE NOTES

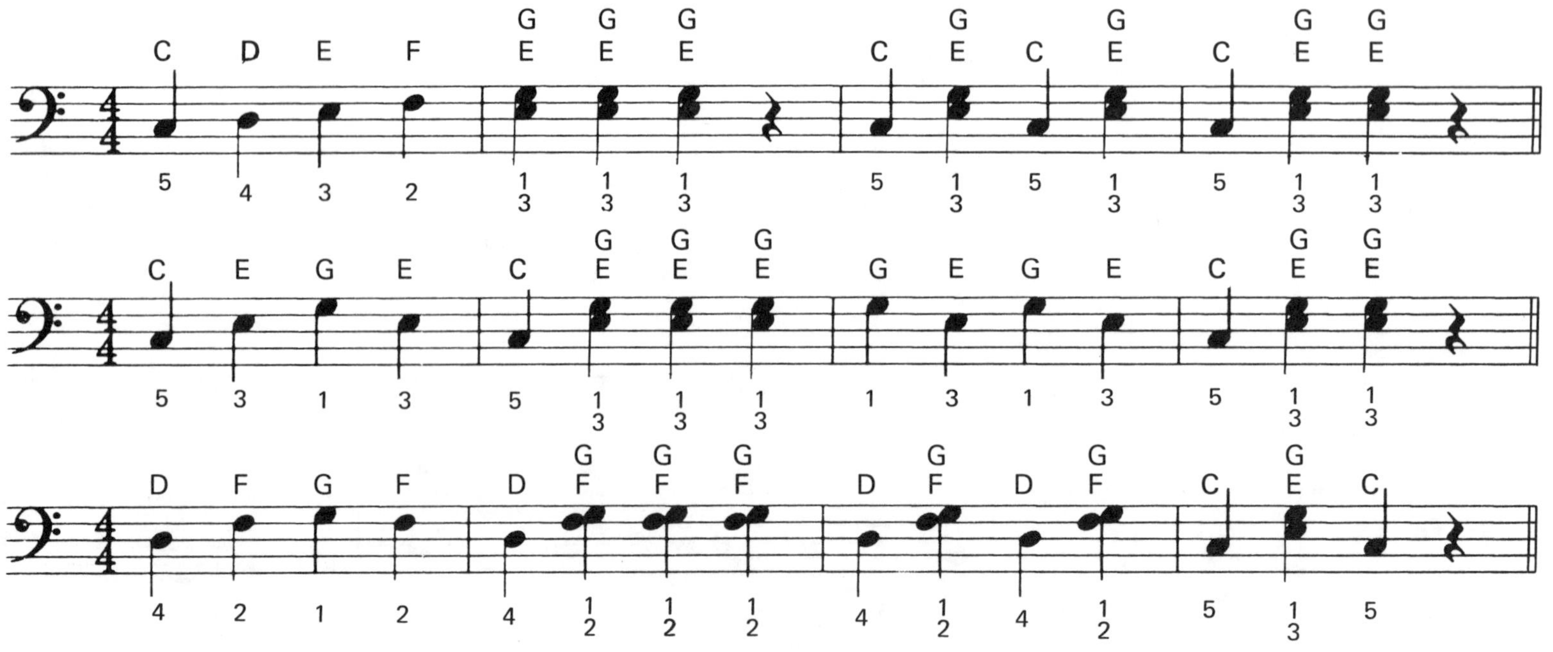

WHOLE NOTE	HALF NOTES	QUARTER NOTES
4 COUNTS	2 COUNTS EACH NOTE	1 COUNT EACH NOTE

WATCH THE MUSIC! NOT THE PIANO.
KEEP YOUR HAND IN A CURLED POSITION.

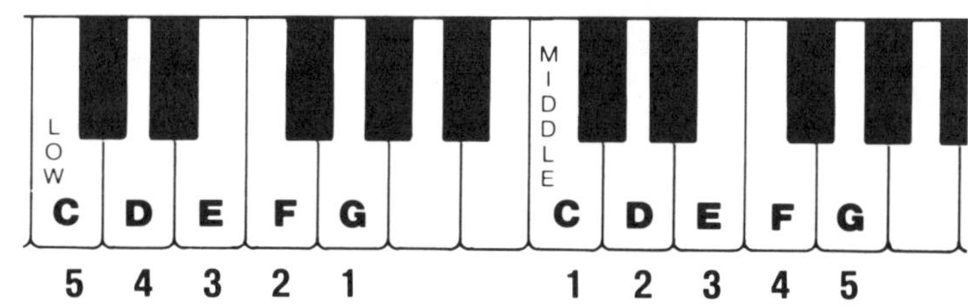

LOVE SOMEBODY

LOVE SOMEBODY

BROTHER JOHN

(Five notes, C-D-E-F-G)

1. RIGHT HAND ONLY

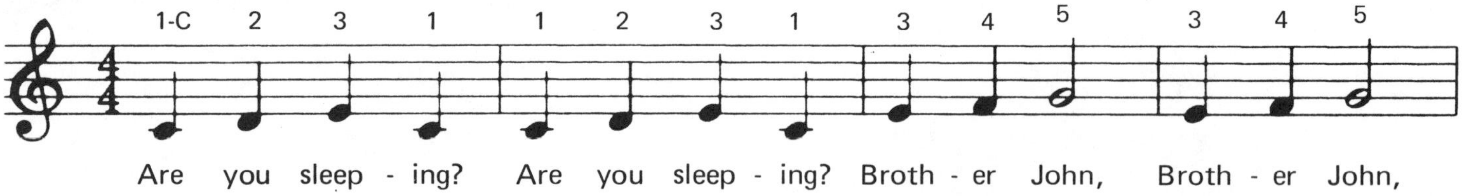
1-C 2 3 1 1 2 3 1 3 4 5 3 4 5
Are you sleep - ing? Are you sleep - ing? Broth - er John, Broth - er John,

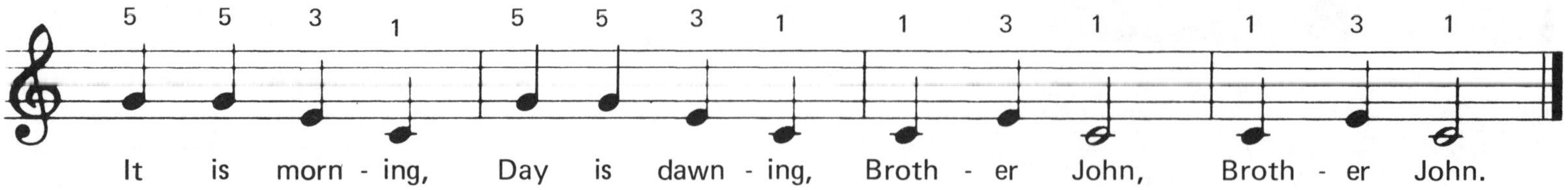
5 5 3 1 5 5 3 1 1 3 1 1 3 1
It is morn - ing, Day is dawn - ing, Broth - er John, Broth - er John.

2. LEFT HAND ONLY

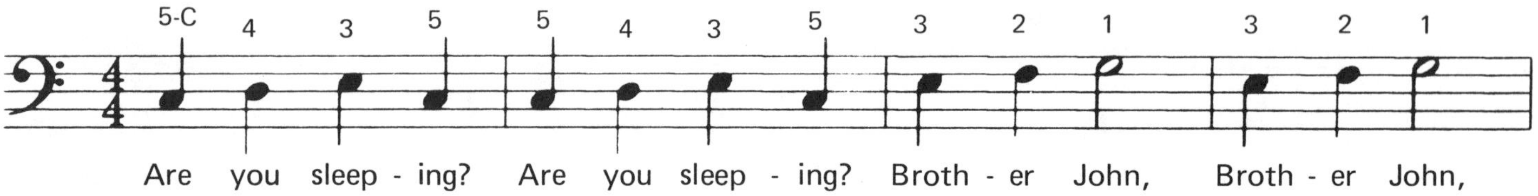
5-C 4 3 5 5 4 3 5 3 2 1 3 2 1
Are you sleep - ing? Are you sleep - ing? Broth - er John, Broth - er John,

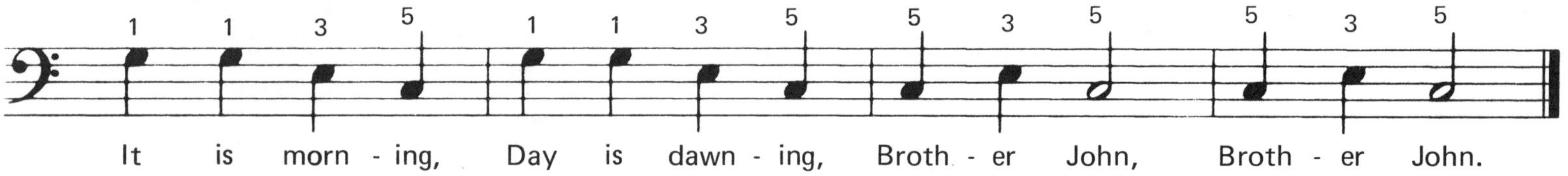
1 1 3 5 1 1 3 5 5 3 5 5 3 5
It is morn - ing, Day is dawn - ing, Broth - er John, Broth - er John.

BROTHER JOHN

3. RIGHT HAND / TOGETHER / LEFT HAND

1-C 2 3 1 1 2 3 1 3 4 5 3 4 5
Are you sleep - ing? Are you sleep - ing? Broth - er John, Broth - er John,
3-E 5 3 5 1 3 1 3

5 5 3 1 5 5 3 1 1 3 1 1 3 1
It is morn - ing, Day is dawn - ing, Broth - er John, Broth - er John.
3 5 3 5 1 3 1 3
(Whole note 4 counts.)

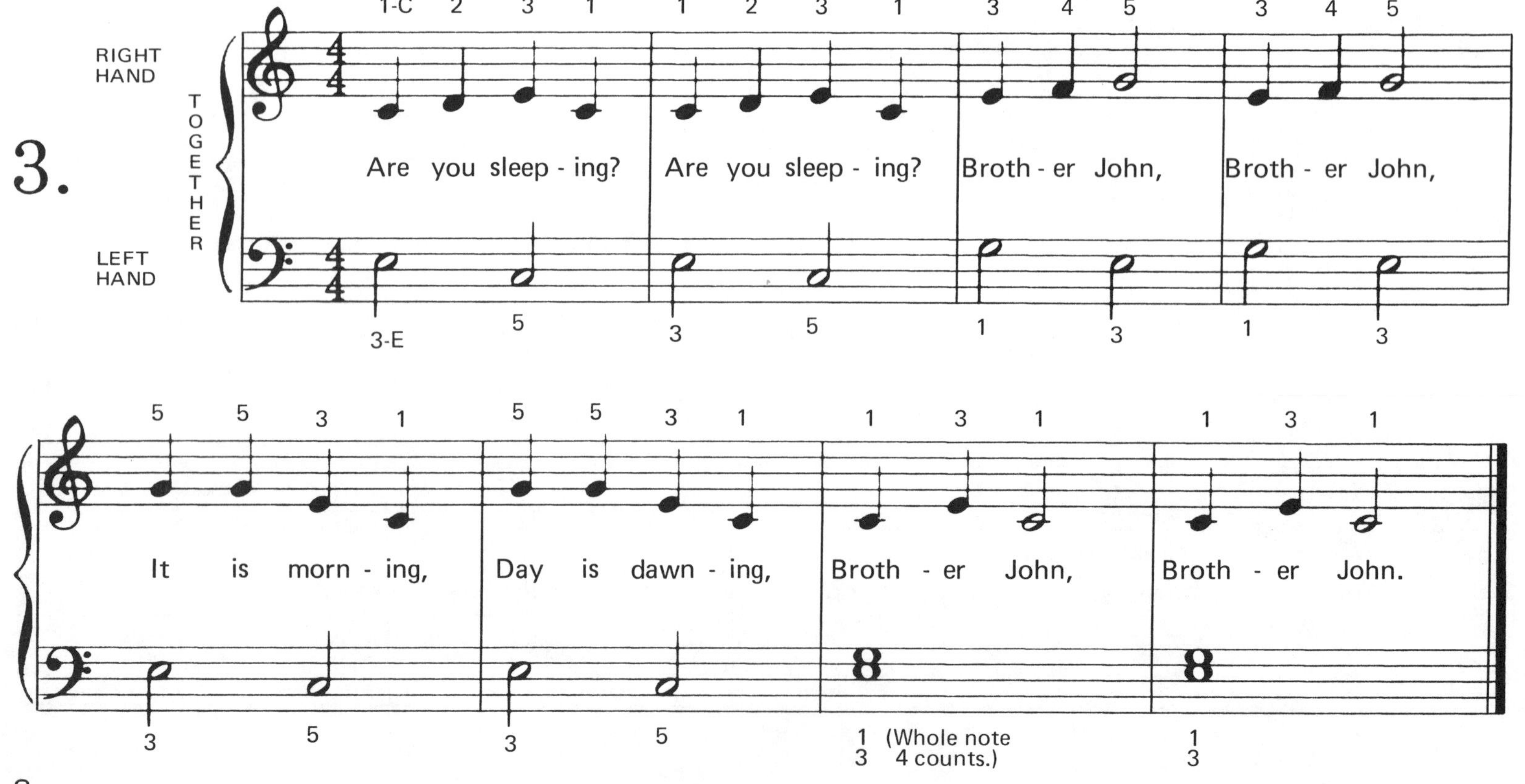

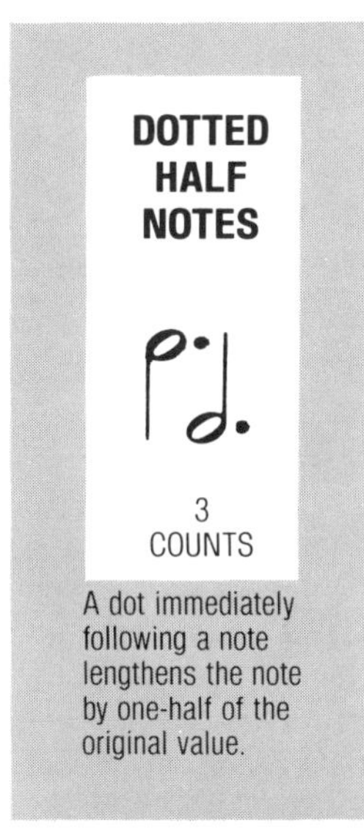

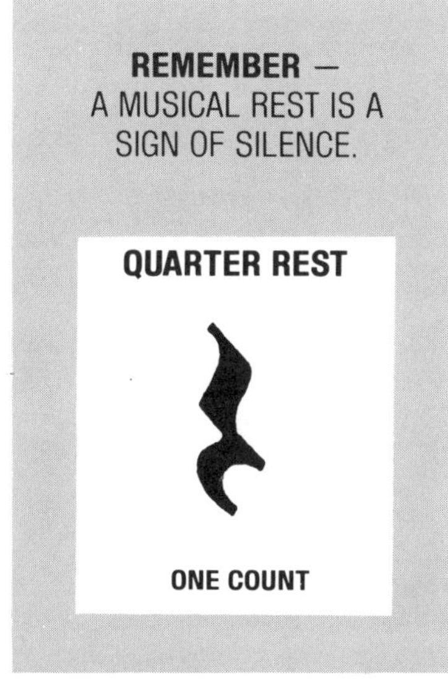

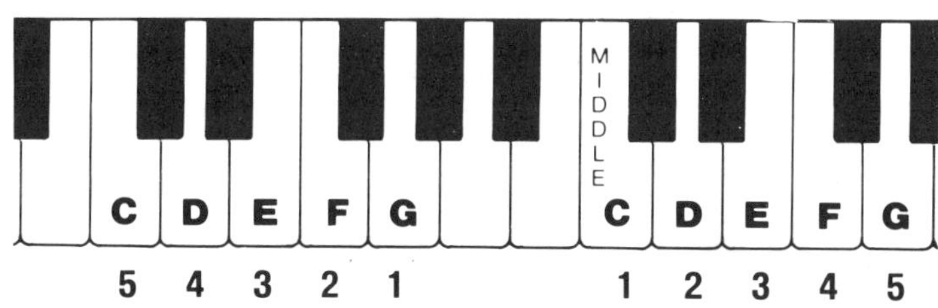

DOTTED HALF NOTES

3 COUNTS

A dot immediately following a note lengthens the note by one-half of the original value.

REMEMBER – A MUSICAL REST IS A SIGN OF SILENCE.

QUARTER REST

ONE COUNT

MIDDLE
C D E F G
C D E F G
5 4 3 2 1
1 2 3 4 5

DOWN BY THE STATION

(Remember to hold all notes for their full time value.)

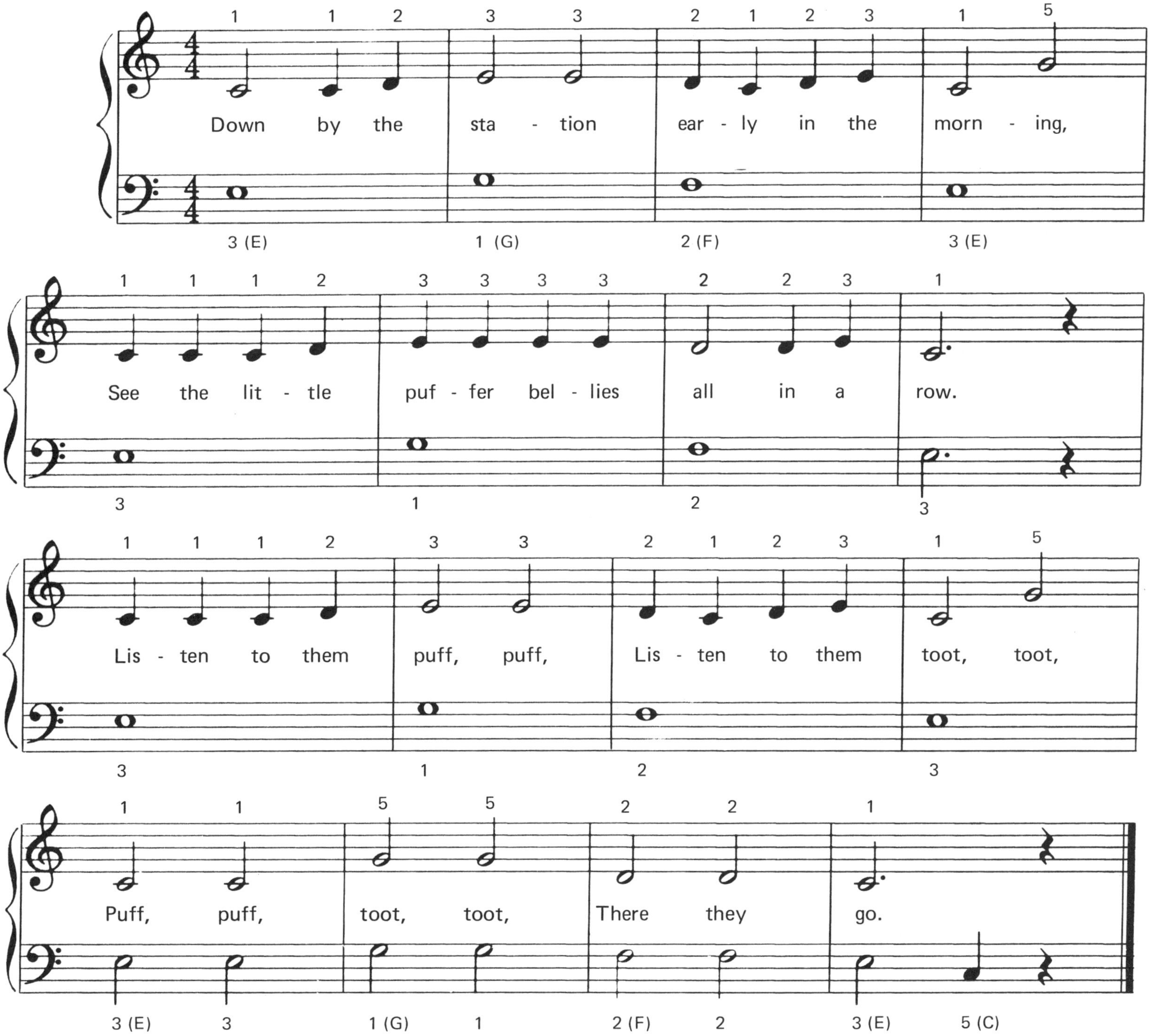

Down by the sta - tion ear - ly in the morn - ing,
See the lit - tle puf - fer bel - lies all in a row.
Lis - ten to them puff, puff, Lis - ten to them toot, toot,
Puff, puff, toot, toot, There they go.

RESTS A musical rest is a sign of silence. The length of silence depends on the shape or style of the rest sign.

HALF MEASURE REST
SITS ON 3RD LINE
FULL MEASURE REST
HANGS FROM 4TH LINE
QUARTER REST
1 COUNT

FOR EVERY KIND OF NOTE THERE IS A REST OF EQUAL VALUE.

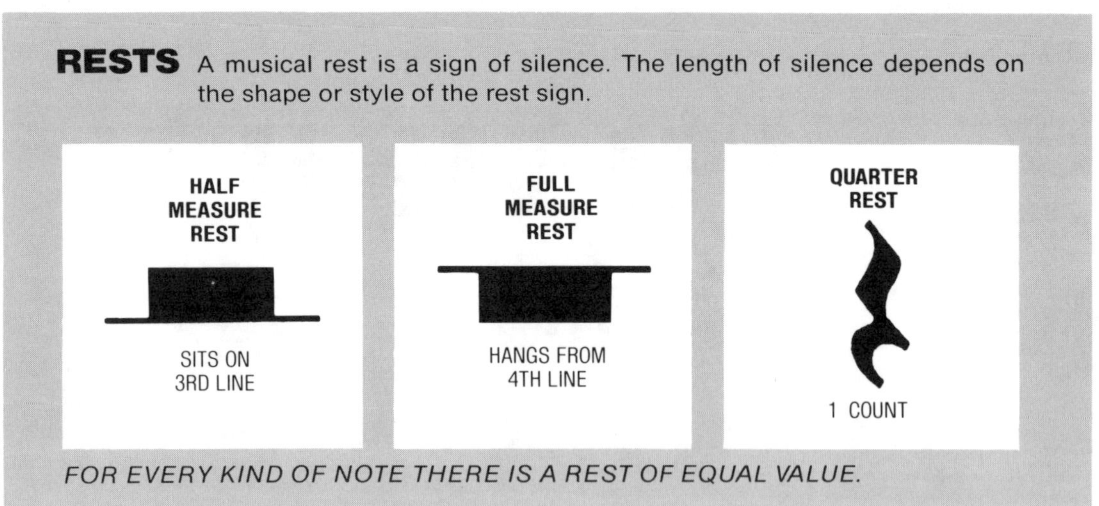

TICK TOCK

FULL MEASURE REST FOR RIGHT HAND
4 counts
4 counts
FULL MEASURE REST FOR LEFT HAND
Quarter rest 1 count
Half measure rest (2 counts)

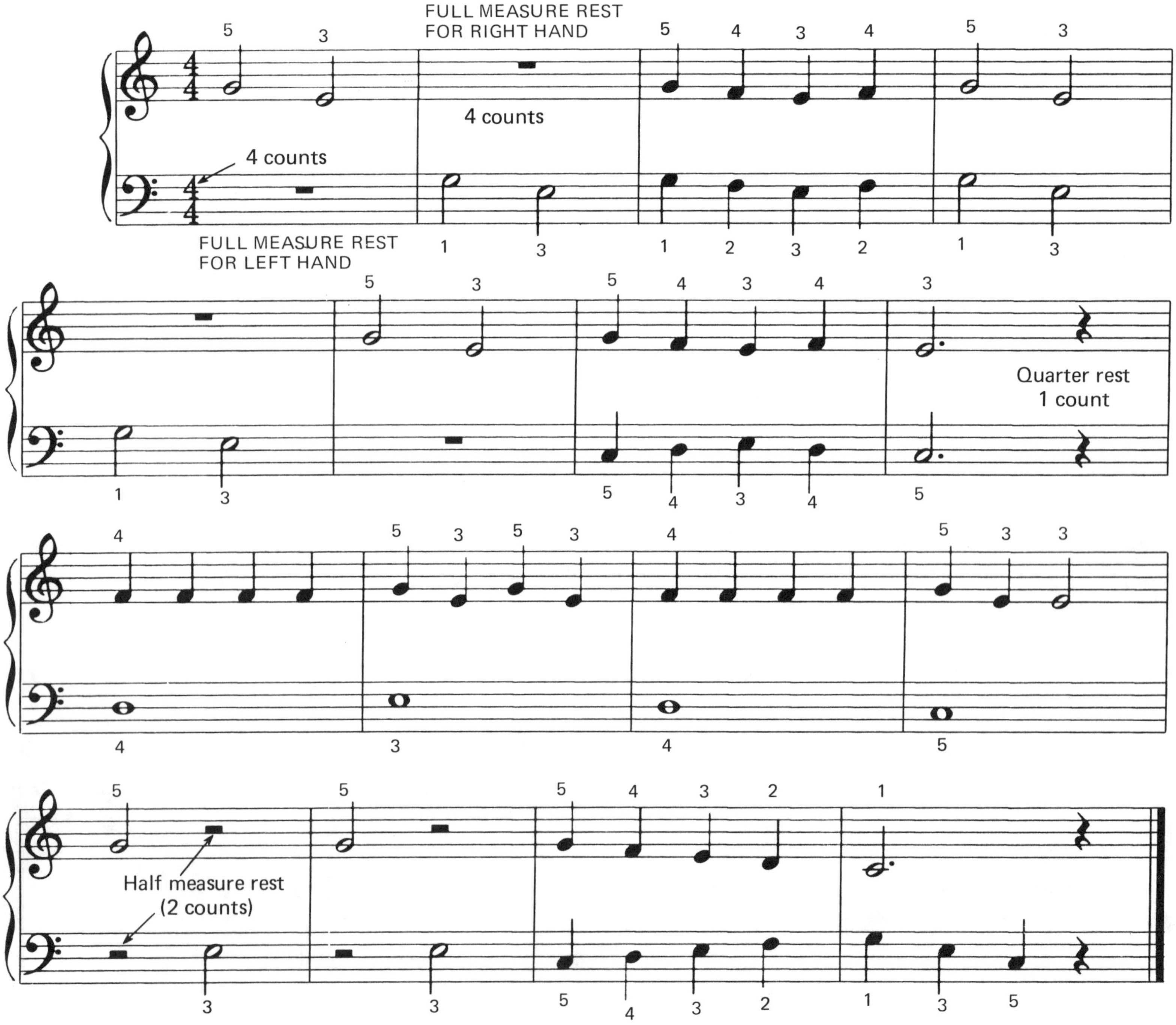

SHARP

RAISES THE PITCH OF A NOTE BY ONE HALF-STEP.

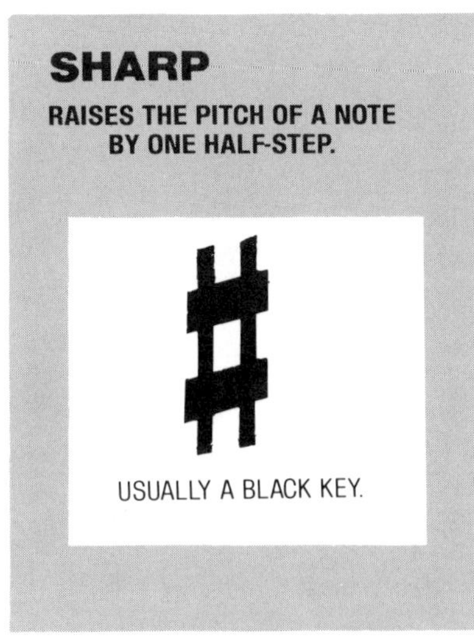

NATURAL

CANCELS A PREVIOUS SHARP OR FLAT AND RESTORES A NOTE TO ITS USUAL PITCH.

ACCIDENTALS

ARE FLATS OR SHARPS THAT OCCUR IN A PIECE BUT ARE NOT A PART OF THE KEY SIGNATURE. THEY ONLY AFFECT THE MEASURE IN WHICH THEY ARE PLACED.

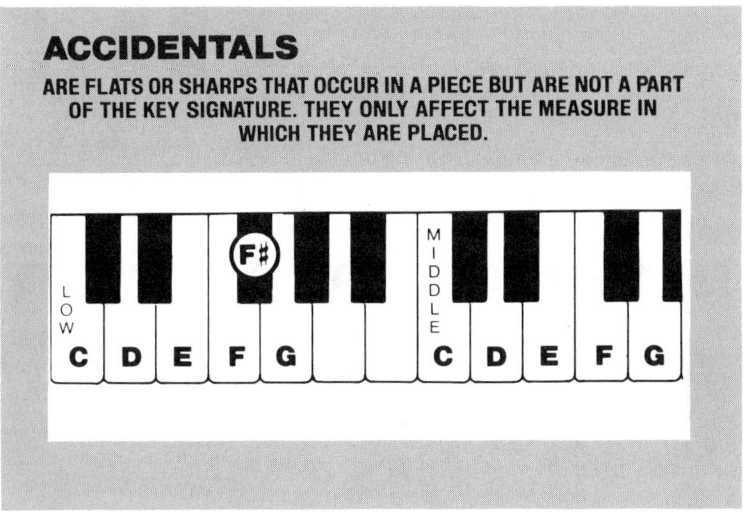

ODE TO JOY

BEETHOVEN (modified)

F♯ Black key

F♮ White key

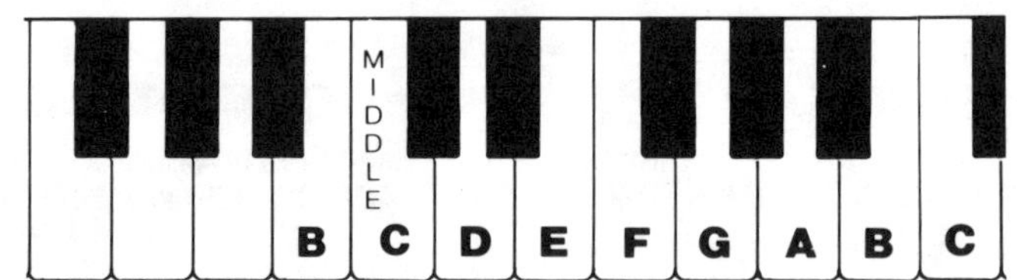

EXTENSION STUDY FOR THE RIGHT HAND

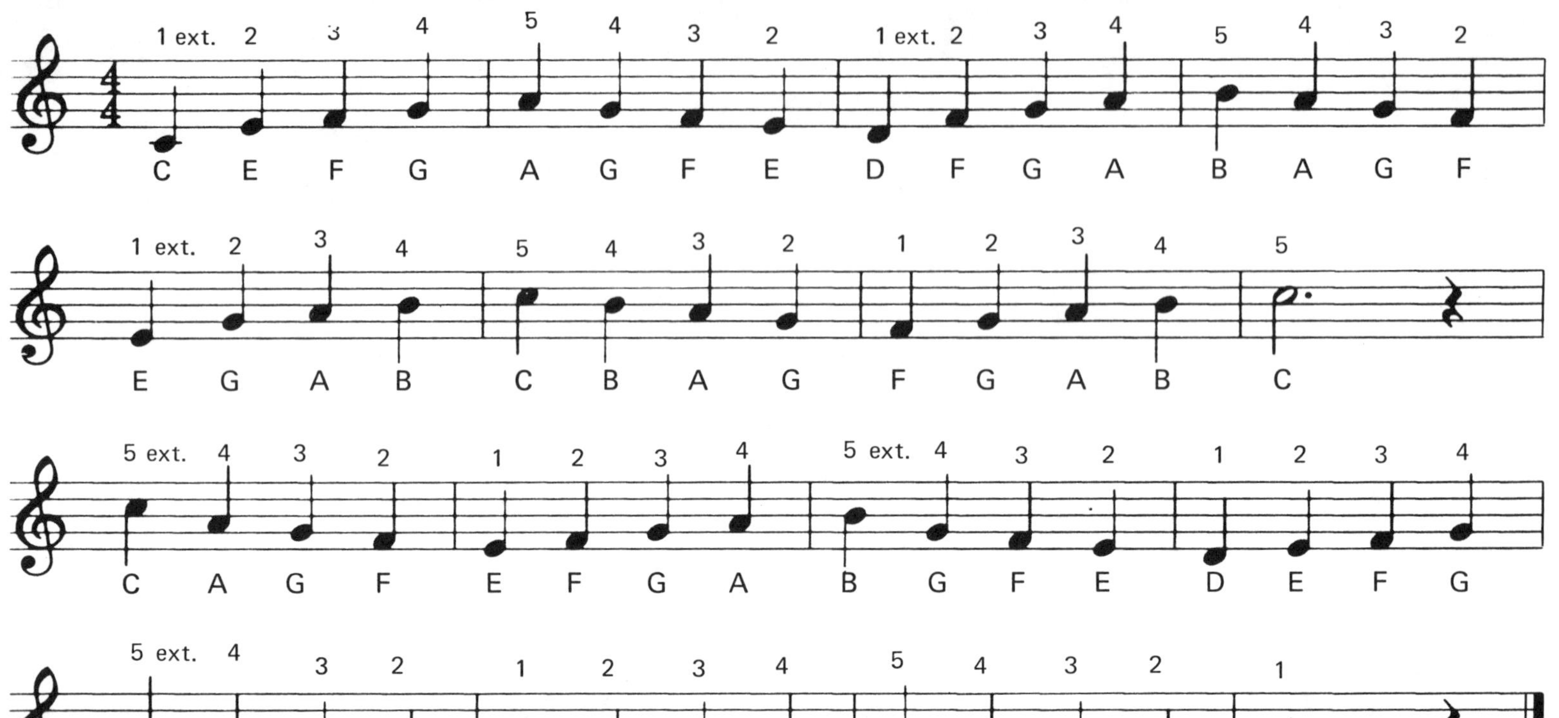

CONTRACTION STUDY FOR THE RIGHT HAND

CONTRACTION STUDY FOR THE LEFT HAND

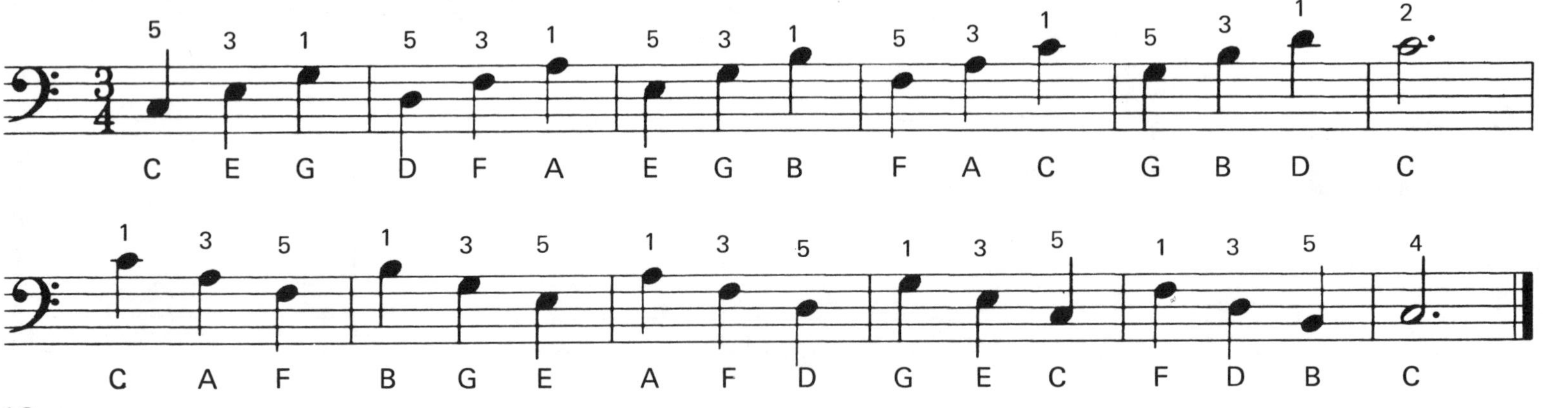

C CHORD
LOW
C E G
5 3 1
5 3 1 1 3 5
F CHORD
MIDDLE
F A C
5 3 1
5 3 1 1 3 5
G CHORD
MIDDLE
G B C D
5 3 1
5 3 1 1 3 5

MIDDLE
C D E F G A B C D

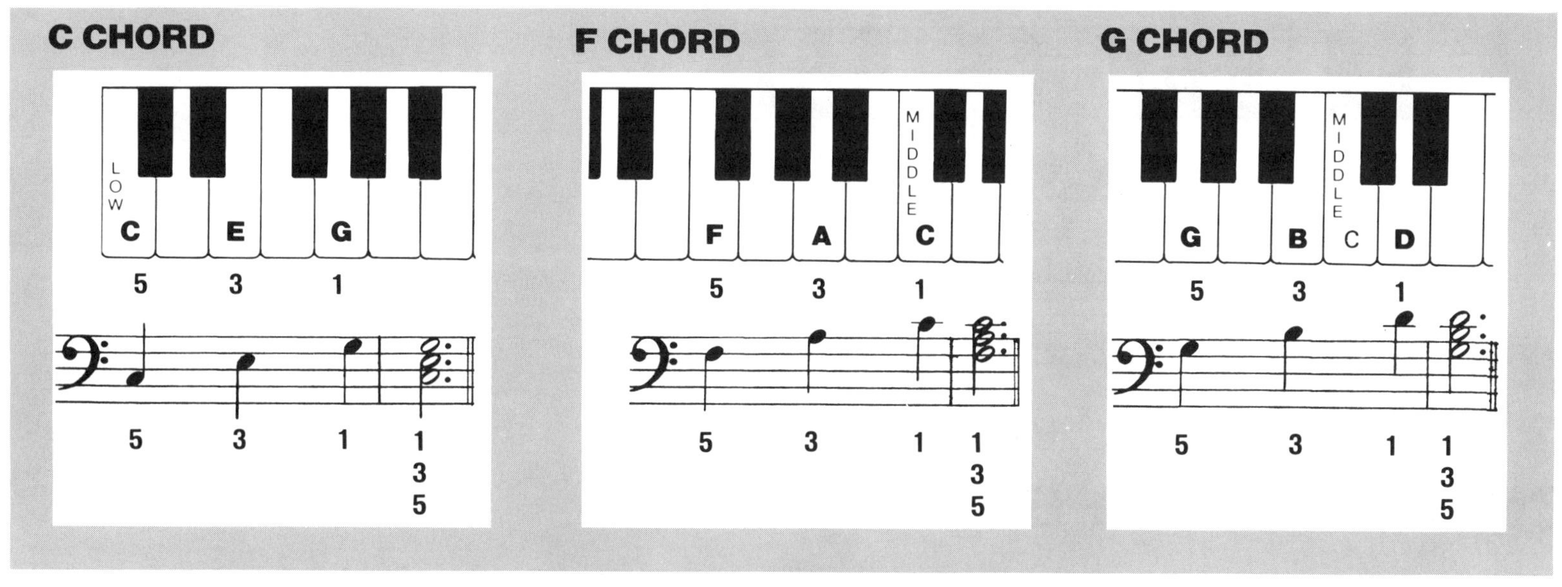

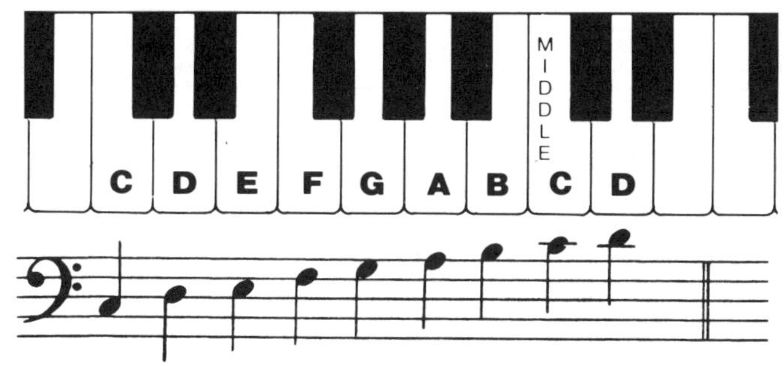

MAJOR TRIADS

A MAJOR TRIAD IS COMPOSED OF THE FIRST, THIRD, AND FIFTH NOTES OF THE SCALE. THE FIRST NOTE IS CALLED THE ROOT.

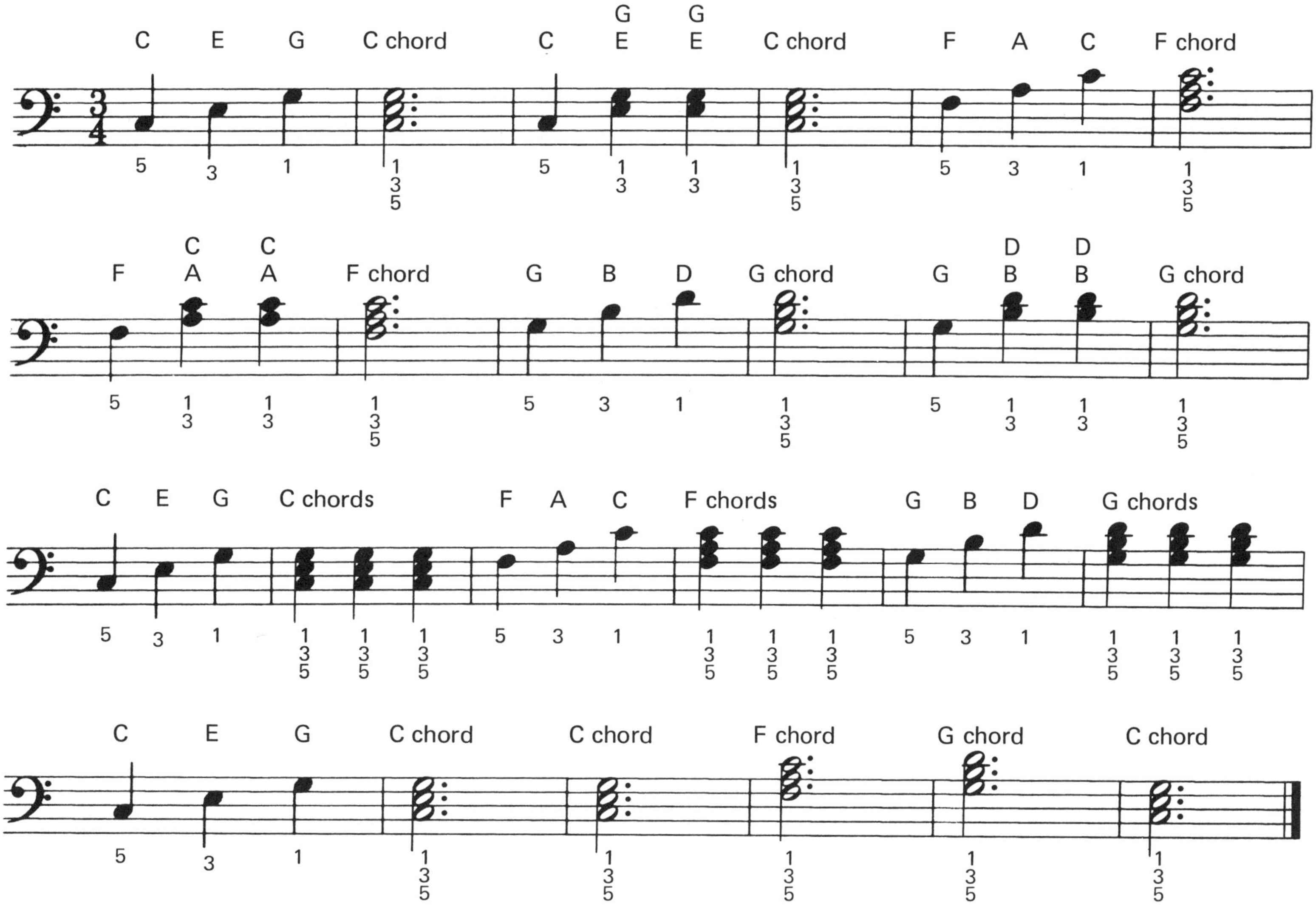

C E G C chord C G E G E C chord F A C F chord
5 3 1 1 3 5 5 1 3 1 3 1 3 5 5 3 1 1 3 5
F C A C A F chord G B D G chord G D B D B G chord
5 1 3 1 3 1 3 5 5 3 1 1 3 5 5 1 3 1 3 1 3 5
C E G C chords F A C F chords G B D G chords
5 3 1 1 3 5 1 3 5 1 3 5 5 3 1 1 3 5 1 3 5 1 3 5 5 3 1 1 3 5 1 3 5 1 3 5
C E G C chord C chord F chord G chord C chord
5 3 1 1 3 5 1 3 5 1 3 5 1 3 5 1 3 5

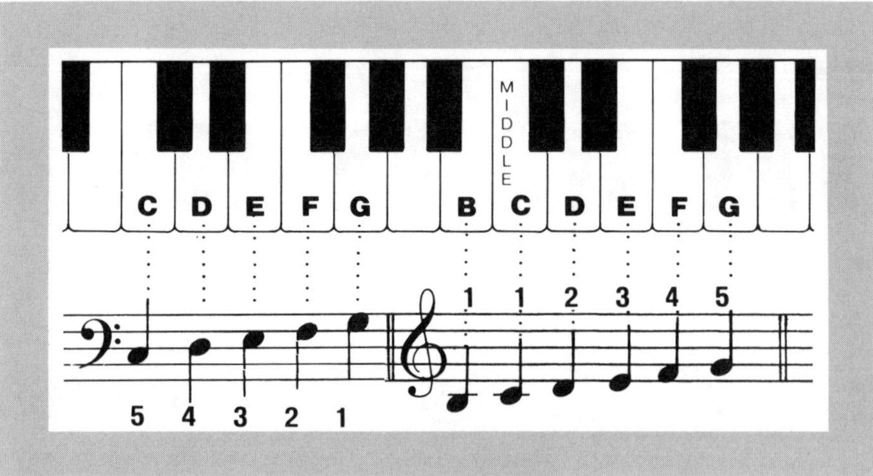

CHERRIES RIPE

Cher - ries ripe, cher - ries ripe, Who will buy my cher - ries ripe?

Ber - ries red, ber - ries red, Who will buy my ber - ries red?

Cher - ries ripe, cher - ries ripe, Who will buy my cher - ries ripe?

(LEFT HAND MELODY)

Ber - ries red, ber - ries red, Who will buy my ber - ries red?

INCOMPLETE MEASURES

The top number of the time signature indicates the number of counts in each FULL measure of a composition. The first and last measures may not be complete but the total count will make a full measure. When the first measure does not contain the number of counts shown in the time signature, the remaining counts will be found in the final measure.

COCKLES AND MUSSELS

KEY OF F MAJOR

The signature for the key of F is one flat (B♭). In this key all B's are played one half step lower. Play the first black key to the left. If B natural is needed it will be shown with the usual natural sign. (♮) The natural sign will cancel B♭ for that one measure or possibly only a part of the measure.

FLAT

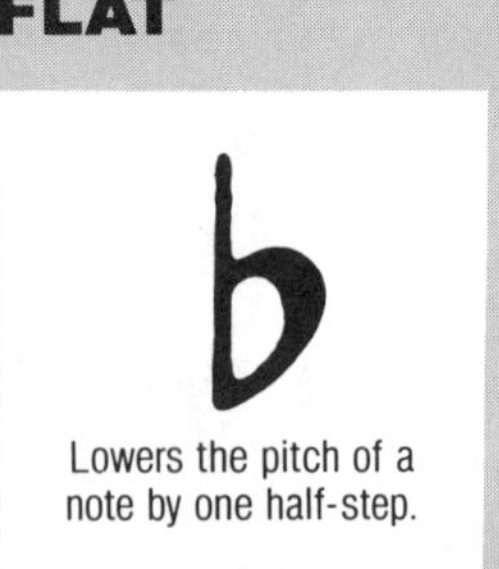

Lowers the pitch of a note by one half-step.

NATURAL

Cancels a previous sharp or flat and restores a note to its usual pitch.

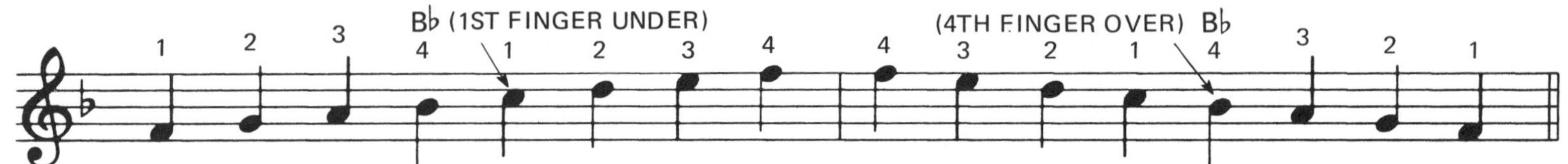

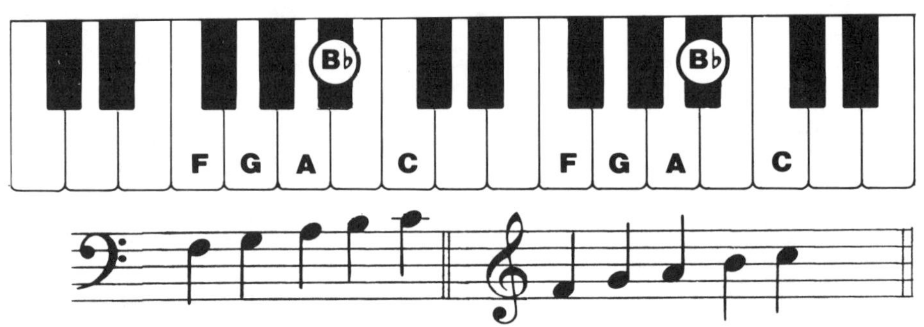

RING, RING THE BANJO (Key of F. Watch for B♭.)

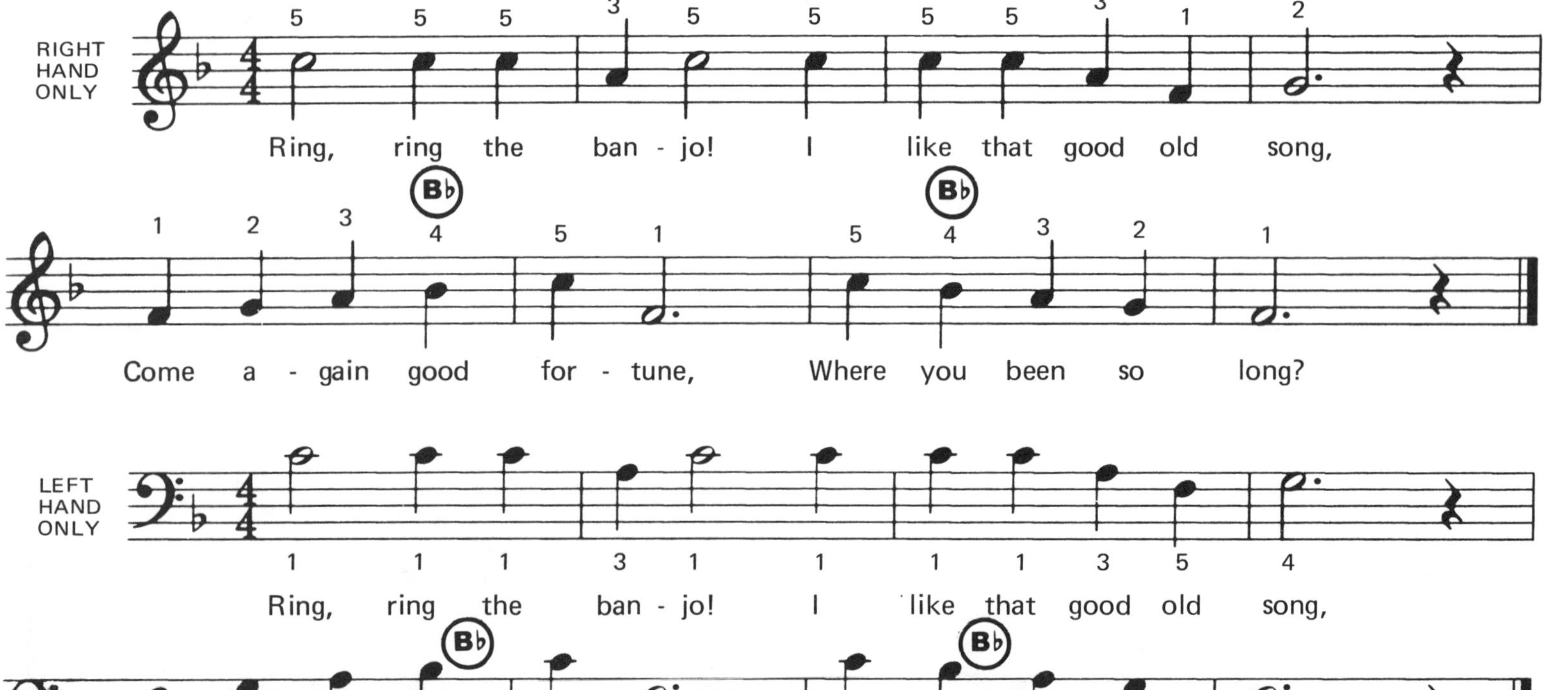

KEY AND TIME SIGNATURE

TIED NOTES

A TIE (⌒) OR (‿) is a curved line uniting two or more notes of the same pitch (same line or space). The tone is sustained (held) for the total value of the tied notes.

LEFT HAND PREPARATORY WORK

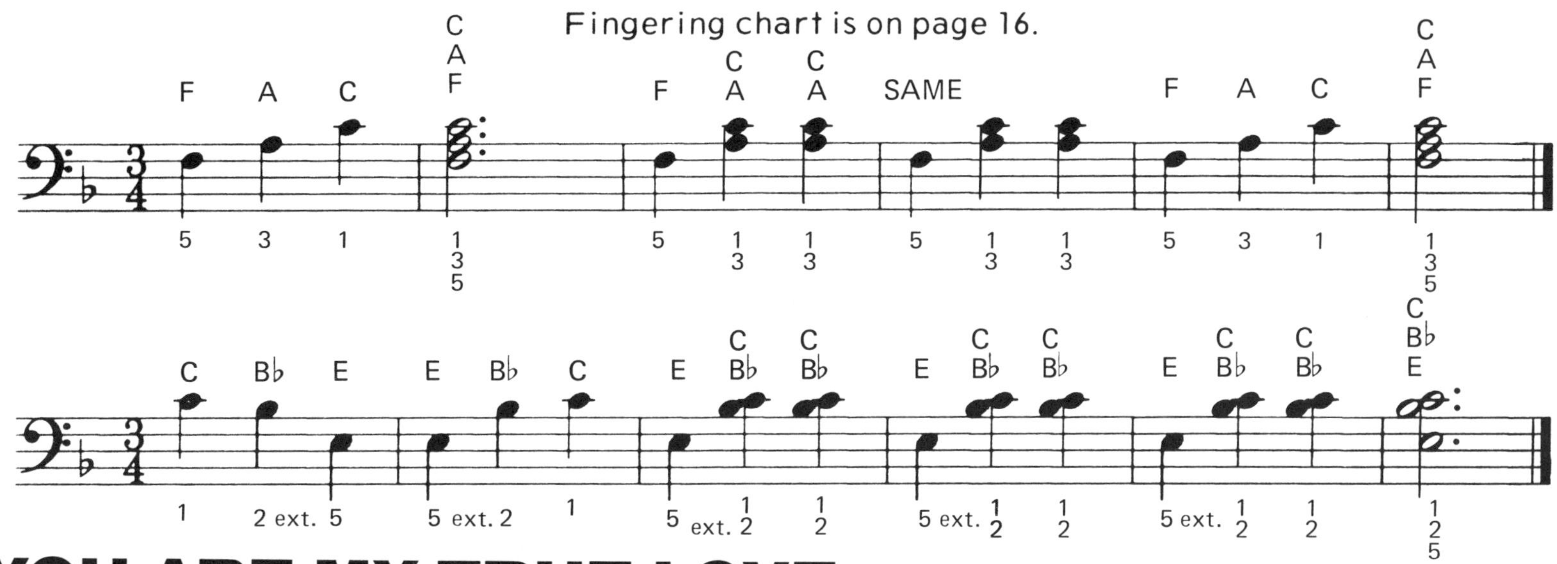

YOU ARE MY TRUE LOVE

(Key of F. Watch for B♭.)

3-A 3 3 2 3 5 4-B♭ 2
5-F 1 3 1 3 5-E 1 2 1 2

2 2 5 4 3 3 3
5-E 1 2 1 2 5-F 1 3 1 3

3 2 3 5 4 2 3 4 5 4 2 1 (TIED NOTES)
5 1 3 1 3 5 1 2 1 2 4-E 1 2 1 2 5 1 3 1 3 1 3 5

INTERVALS

An Interval is the distance from one tone to another. Intervals are counted on the staff from a lower note to a higher note. Example: A to C is a distance of three notes. This is called a third. A to E is a fifth.

EXAMPLES

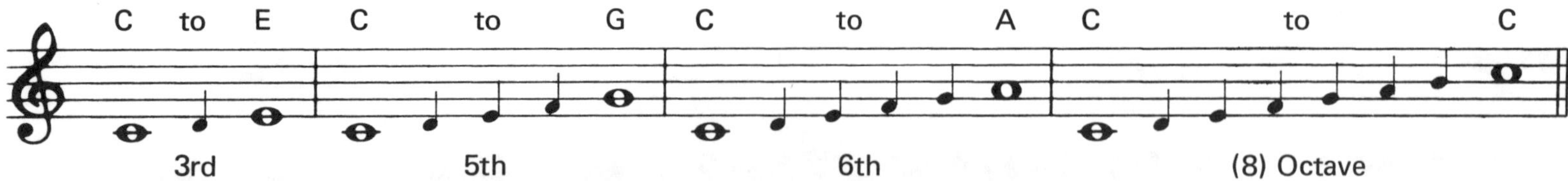

MELODIC INTERVAL

MELODIC INTERVAL

The musical distance between 2 notes played individually.

HARMONIC INTERVAL

MELODIC INTERVALS

HARMONIC INTERVALS

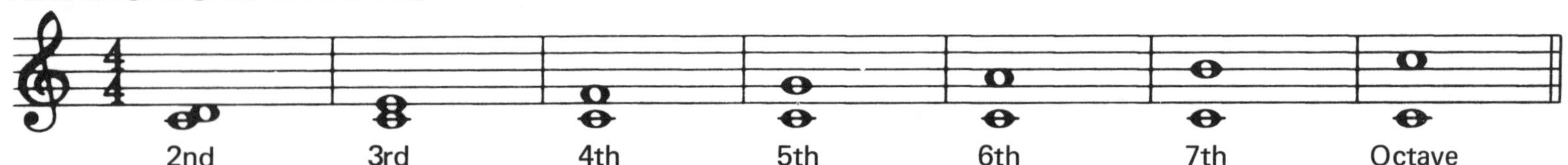

INTERVALS BEYOND THE OCTAVE

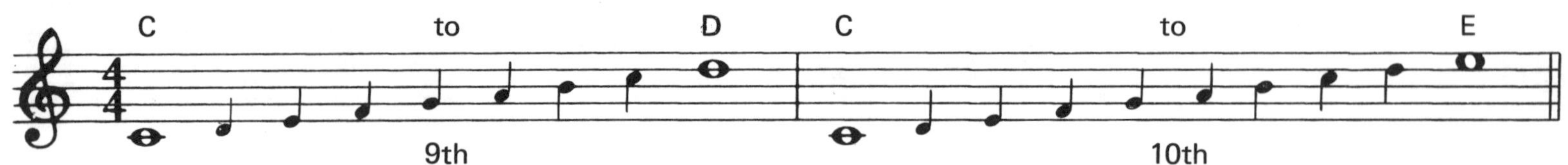

THIRDS

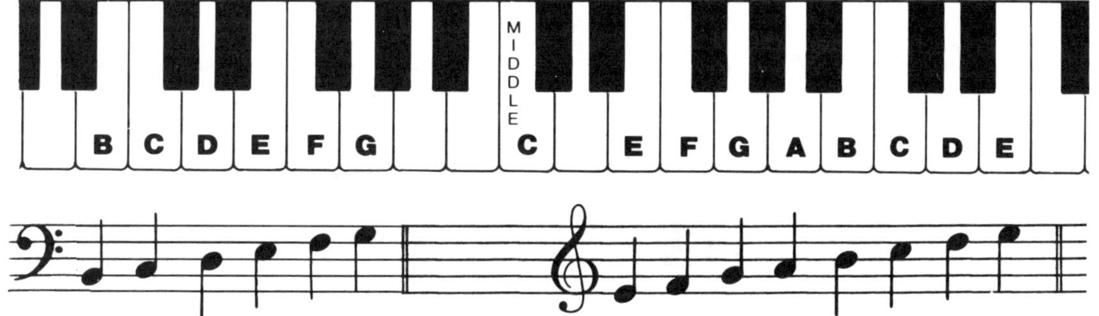

CATHEDRAL CHIMES (RIGHT HAND ONLY)

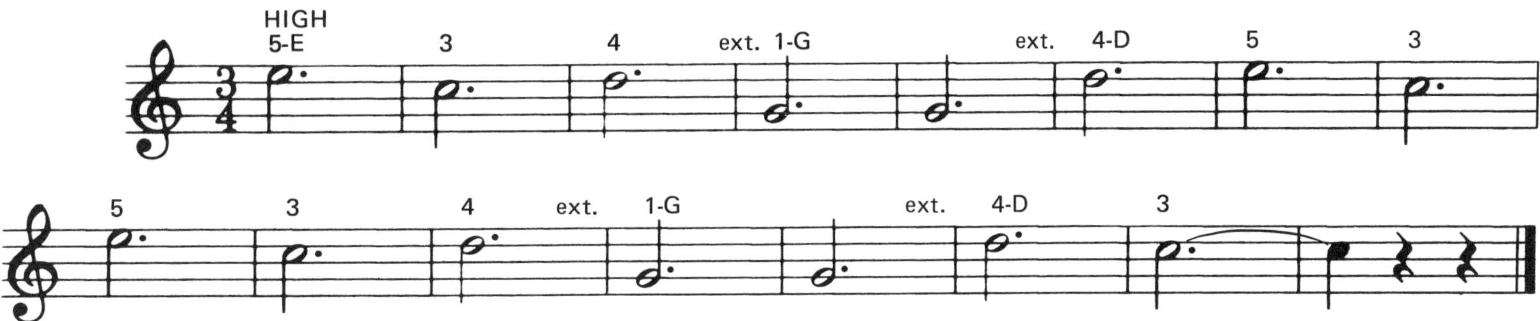

CATHEDRAL CHIMES (USING 6ths)

5-E 1-G
Sixth
3
5-D 1-F
Sixth
2-G
2
5-C 1 3 1 3
5 1 3 1 3
5-B 1 2 1 2
5 1 2 1 2
5 1 2 1 2

5-D 1-F
Sixth
5-E 1-G
Sixth
3
5 1
Sixth
3
5-B 1 2 1 2
5 1 3 1 3
5 1 3 1 3
5 1 3 1 3
5 1 3 1 3

5-D 1-F
Sixth
2-G
2
5-D 1-F
Sixth
5-C 1-E
Sixth
5-B 1 2 1 2
5 1 2 1 2
5 1 2 1 2
5 1 2 1 2
5 1 3 1 3
1 3 5

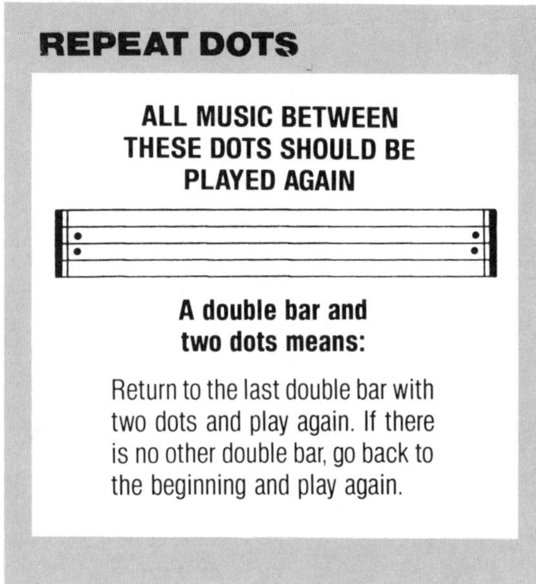

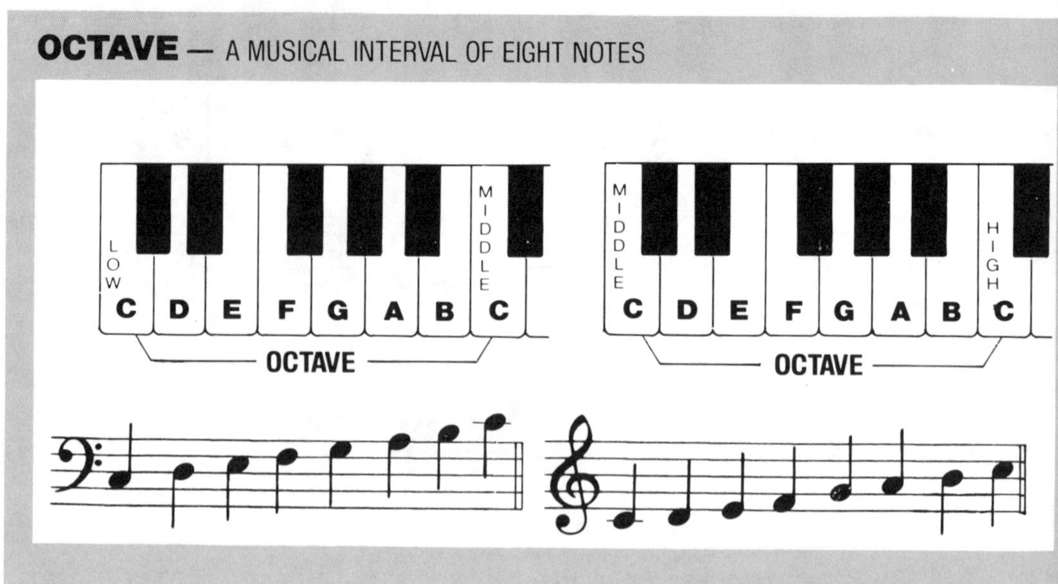

OCTAVE STUDY

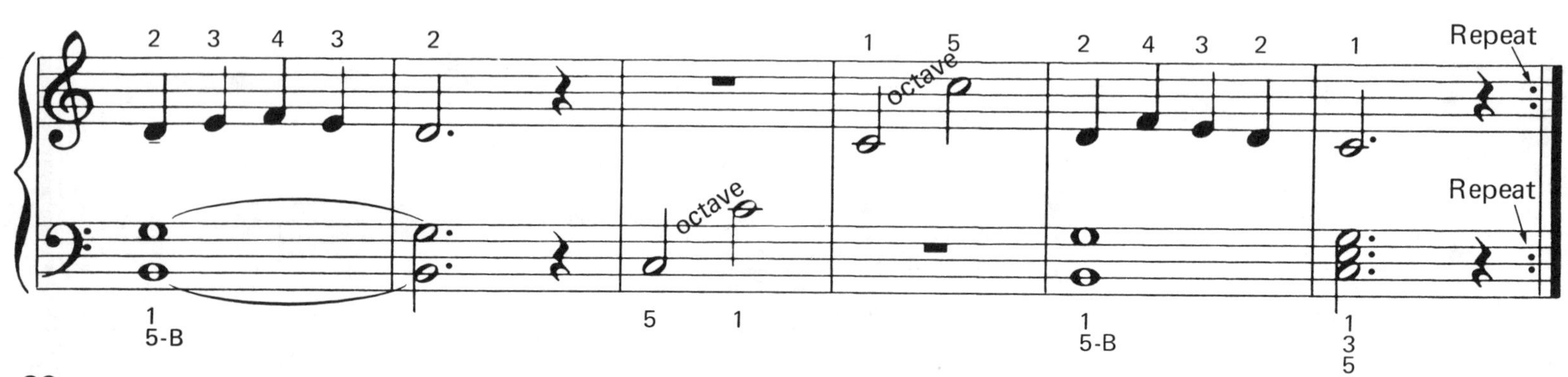

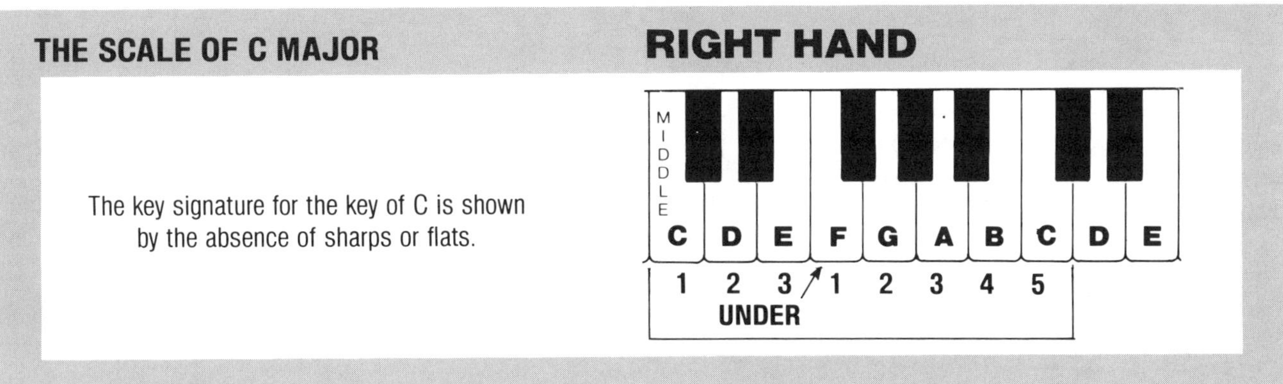

SCALE OF C MAJOR...ONE OCTAVE...BEGINS ON C...ENDS ON C

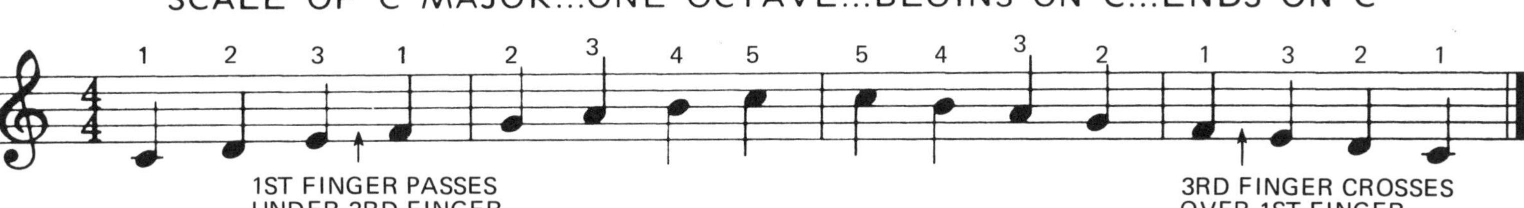

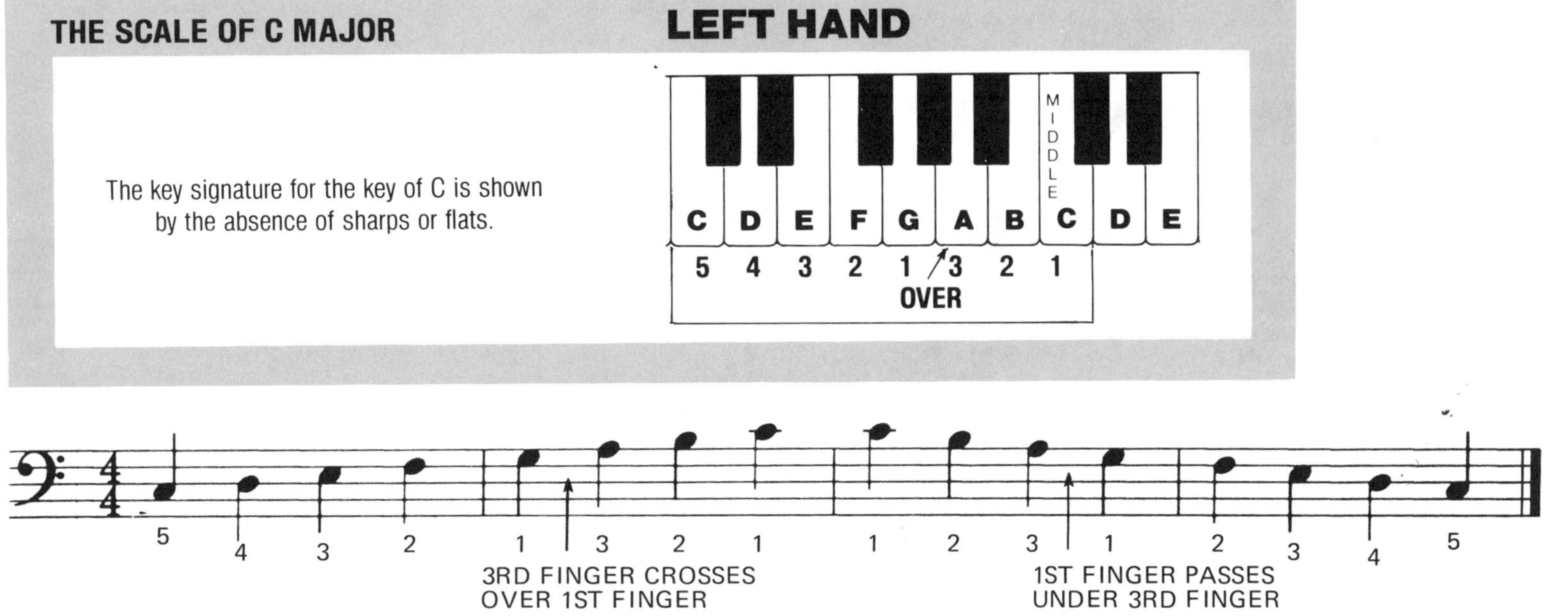

CAN CAN

(RIGHT HAND ONLY)

This familiar melody will provide practice changing fingers and using the C scale in a melodic setting.

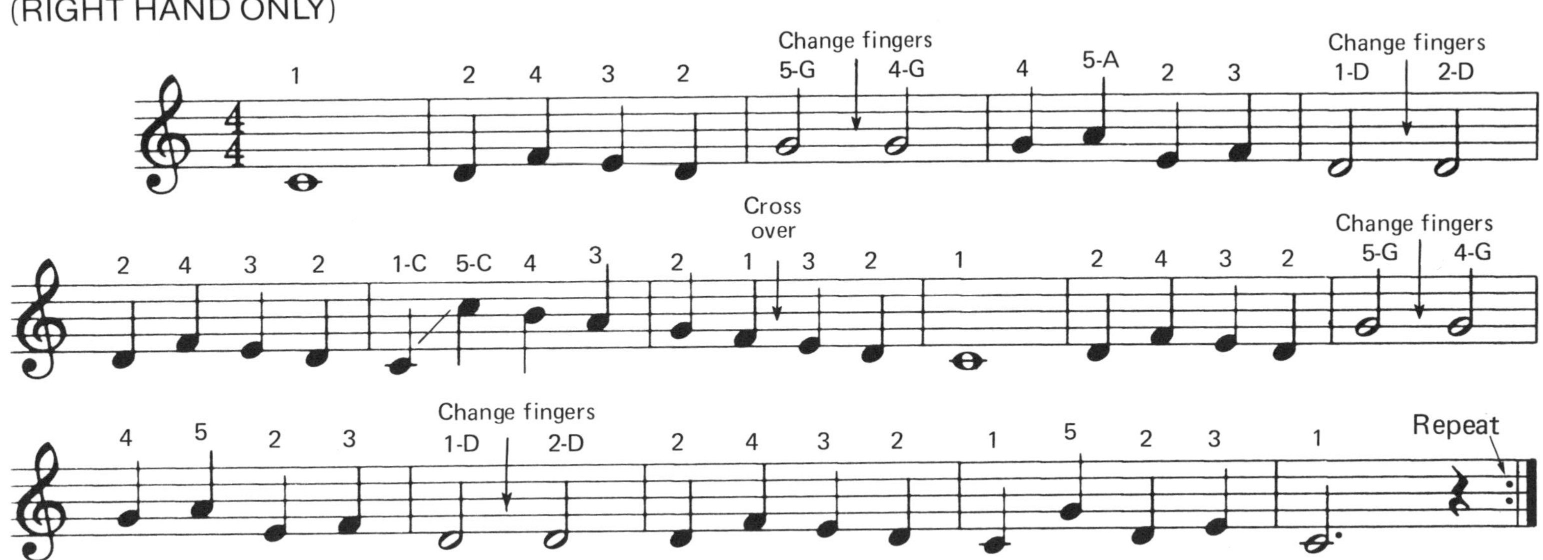

LEGATO

Legato means a group of notes should be played in a smooth and connected manner without stopping between the notes. This may be done by holding down one key until a finger is placed on another.

SLUR

A curved line placed above or below a group of notes to indicate that these notes are to be played in a smooth legato manner.

EXAMPLES OF SLURS AND TIES

(DO NOT PLAY)

Different pitch = Slur
Different lines or spaces.

Same pitch = Tie
Same lines or spaces.

Slur and tie combined.

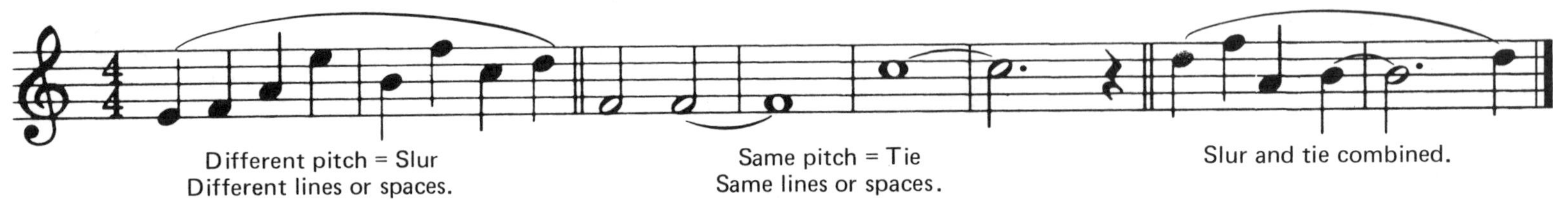

BLACK HAWK WALTZ

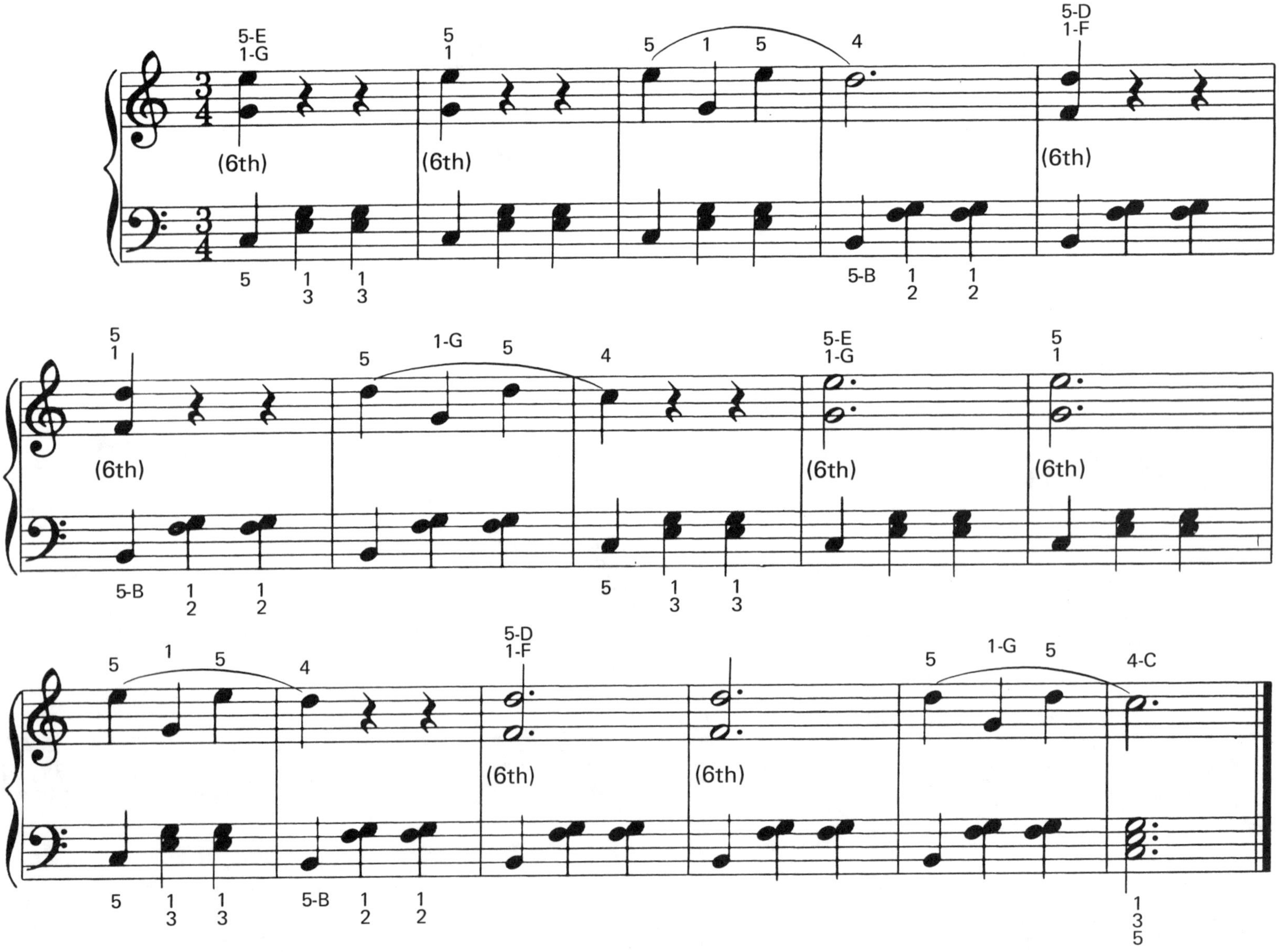

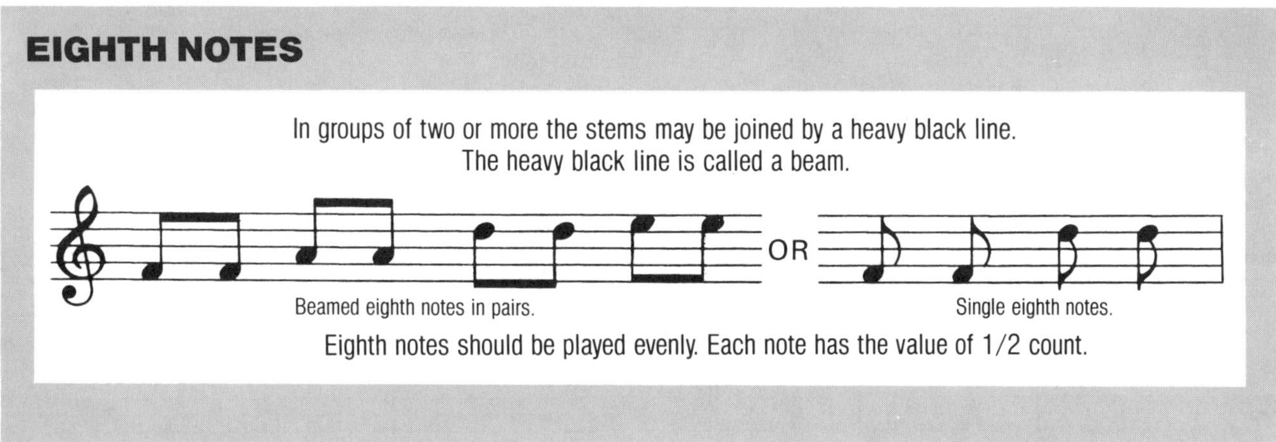

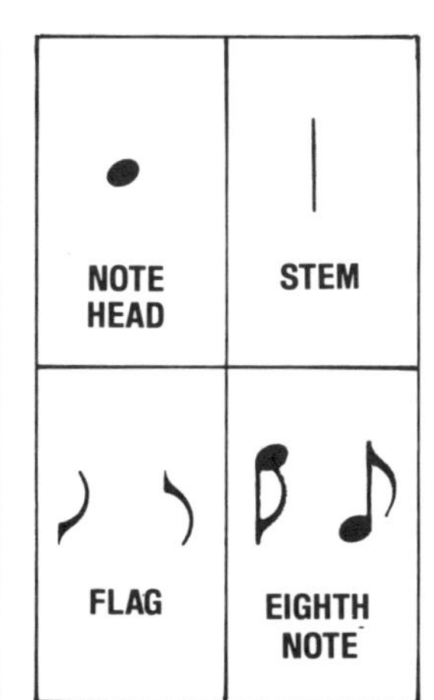

The following excerpts from familiar melodies should be helpful with the eighth notes and the dotted quarter notes. Because the dotted quarter note gets 1-1/2 counts, it is often followed by an eighth note to complete the count.

SHORTNIN' BREAD

BIG ROCK CANDY MOUNTAIN

DOTTED NOTES

VALUE OF THE DOT (•)

A dot immediately following a note lengthens the note by one-half of the original value.

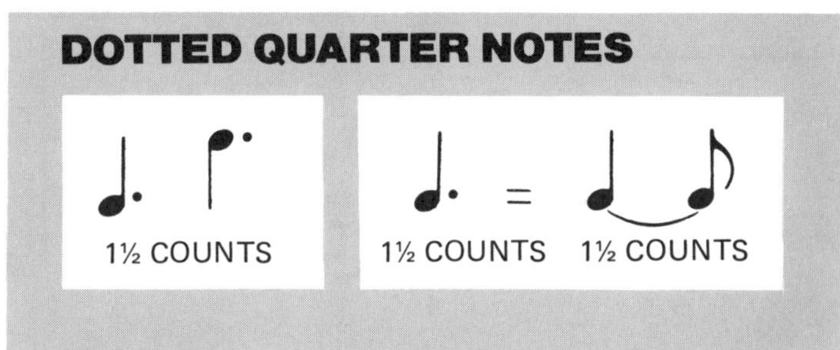

SILENT NIGHT

AMERICA THE BEAUTIFUL

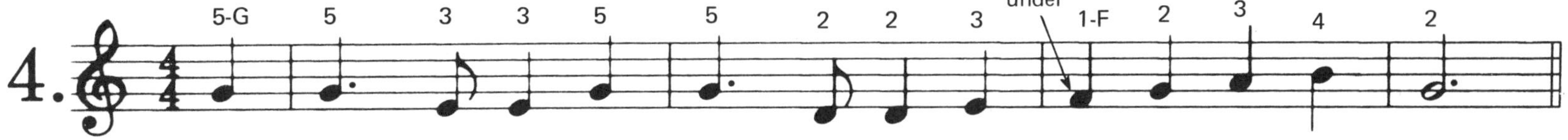

ALOUETTE

Any difficult measure or group of notes that presents a problem should be practiced separately.
Drill on that particular problem until it is mastered.
Some of the measures in Skip To My Lou are shown as examples.

2nd MEASURE
(Right hand)
2nd MEASURE
(Both hands)
4th MEASURE
(Right hand)
4th MEASURE
(Both hands)

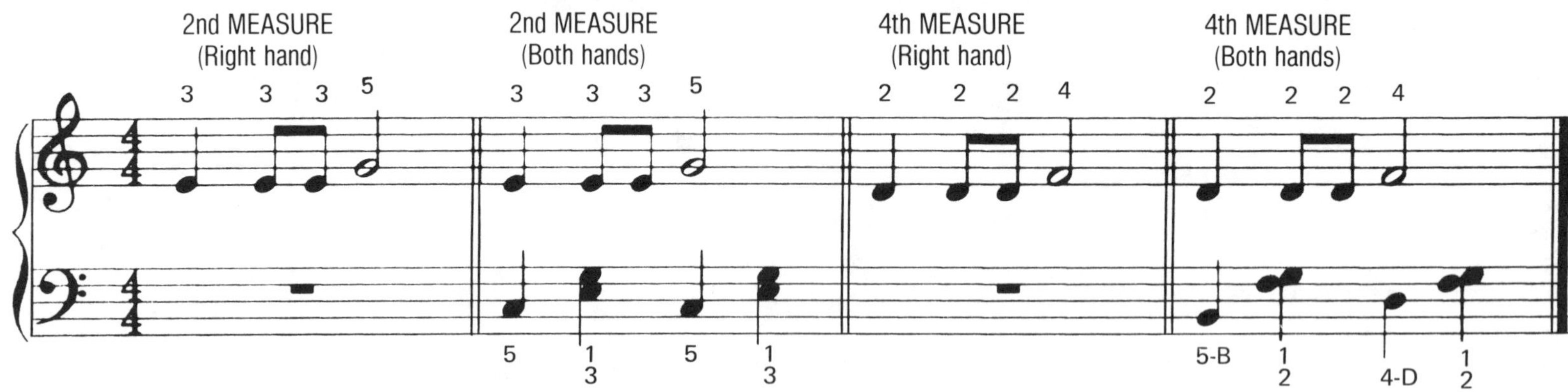

SKIP TO MY LOU

(SQUARE DANCE)

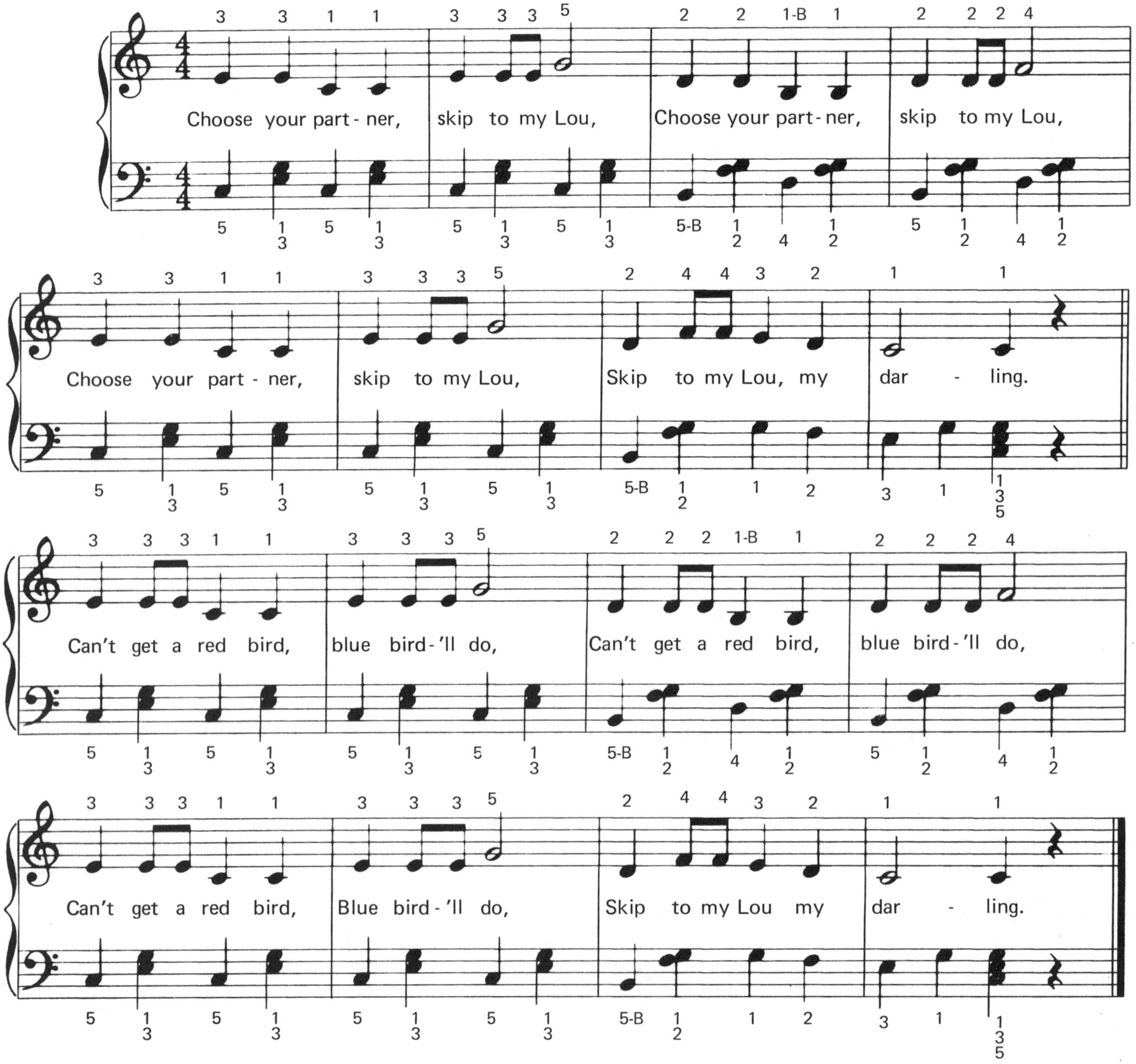

Choose your part - ner, skip to my Lou,
Choose your part - ner, skip to my Lou,
Choose your part - ner, skip to my Lou,
Skip to my Lou, my dar - ling.
Can't get a red bird, blue bird - 'll do,
Can't get a red bird, blue bird - 'll do,
Can't get a red bird, Blue bird - 'll do,
Skip to my Lou my dar - ling.

RITARDANDO

Gradually slowing the tempo or speed. Usually shown as ritard. or rit.

A TEMPO

Return to the normal speed of the music.

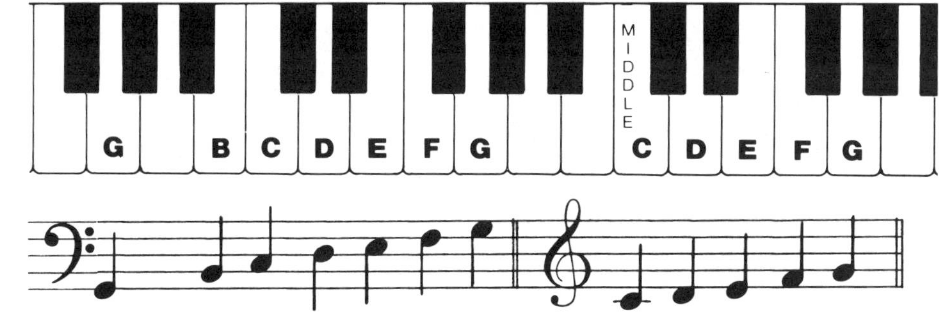

A SONATA BY MOZART

rit.

a tempo

rit.

PREPARATION FOR CUCKOO CLOCK SONG

CUCKOO CLOCK SONG

Cuck - oo, Cuck - oo, The clock strikes the hour of one, Cuck -

oo, Cuck - oo, The clock strikes the hour of two, Cuck -

oo, Cuck - oo, The clock strikes the hour of three, Cuck -

oo, Cuck - oo, The clock strikes the hour of four.

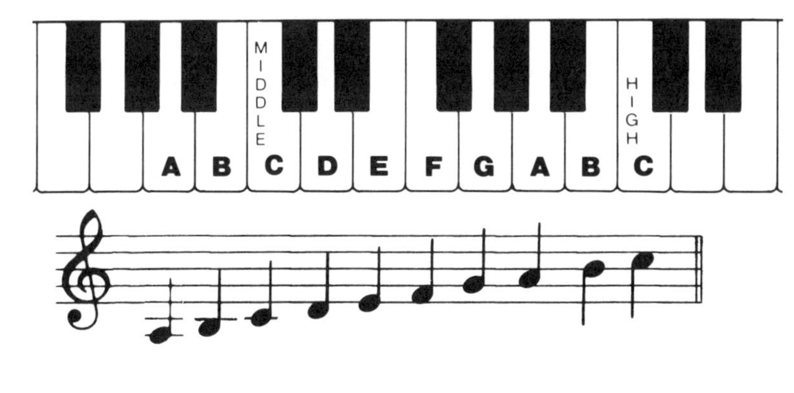

OCTAVE STUDY FOR THE RIGHT HAND

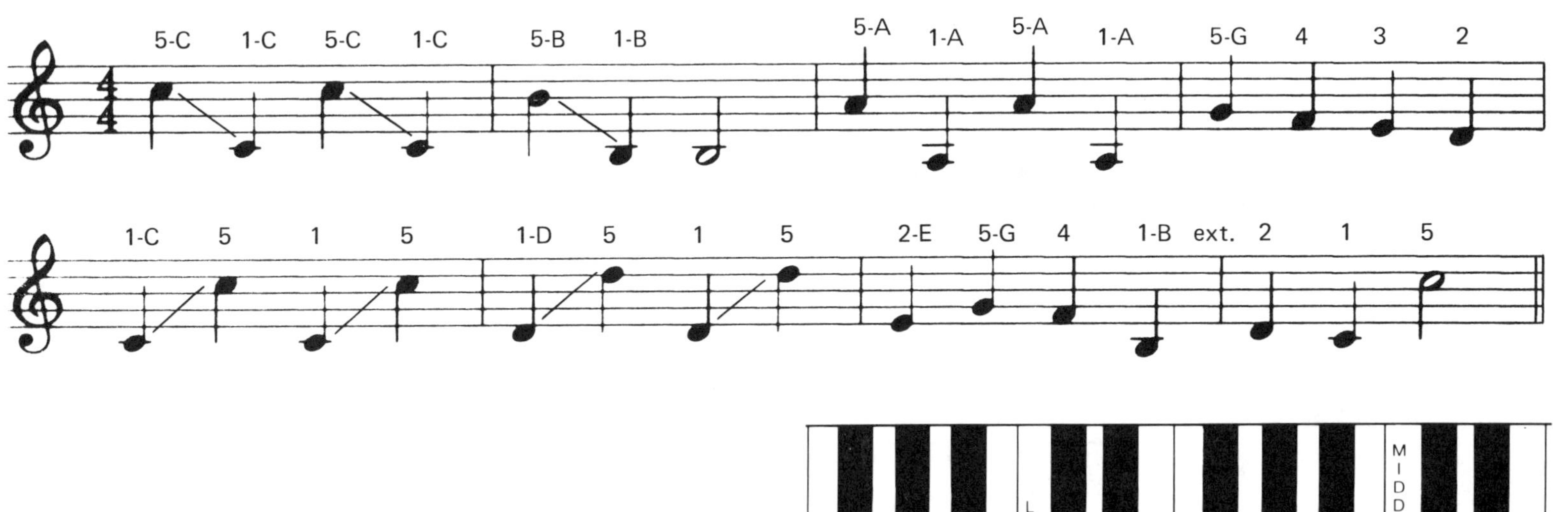

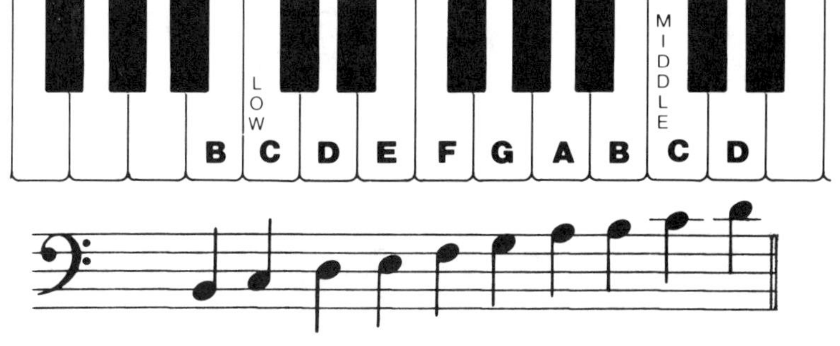

OCTAVE STUDY FOR THE LEFT HAND

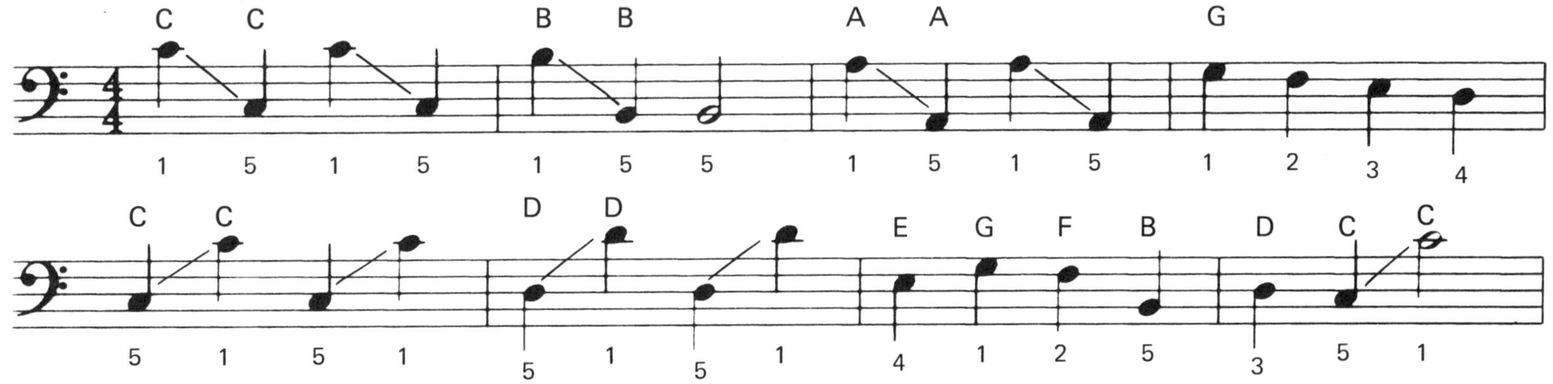

AN EXAMPLE OF THE OCTAVE SIGN

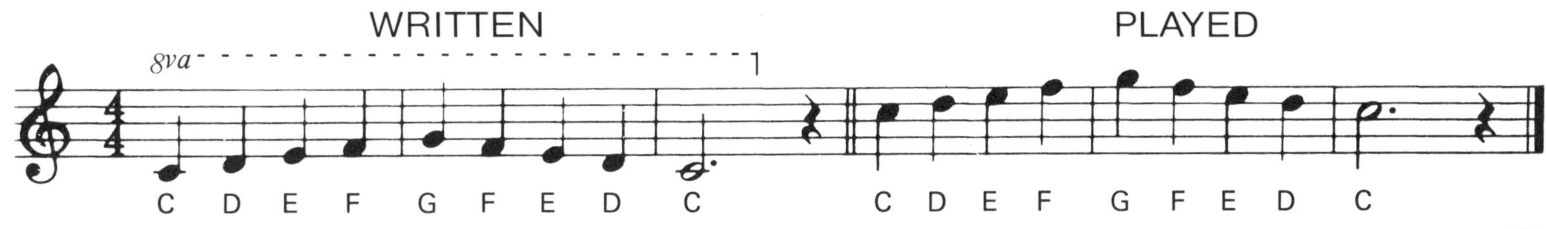

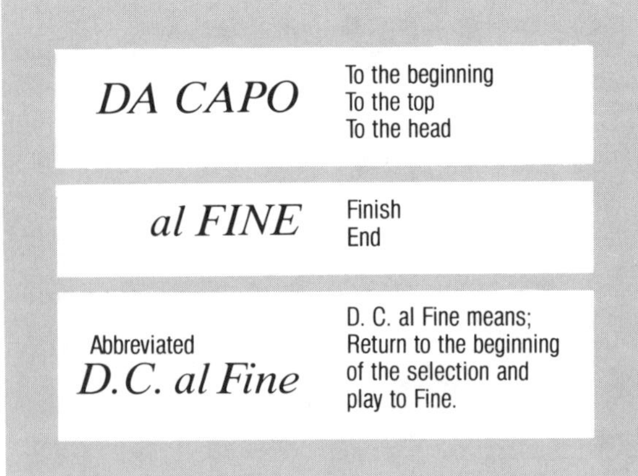

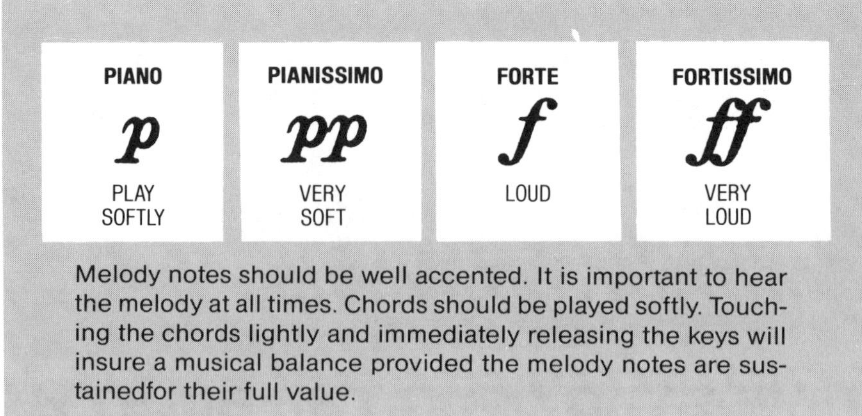

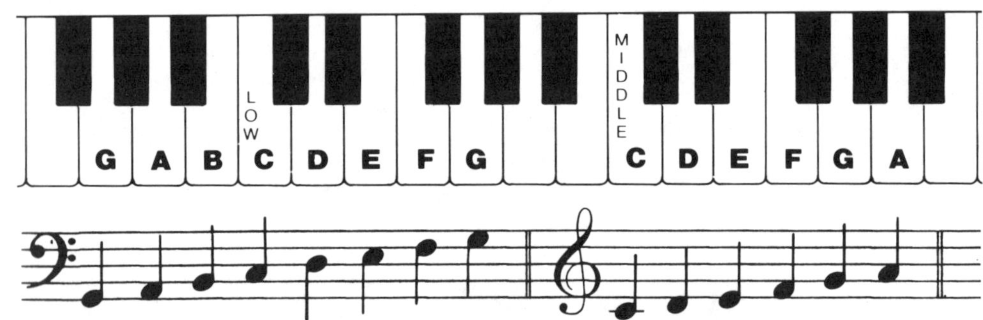

WHEN THE SAINTS GO MARCHING IN

(THIS IS A TWO PAGE SONG)

want to be there with them, When the Saints go
march - ing in. Fine
Oh when the Saints
CHANGE HAND POSITION
go march-ing in, Oh when the Saints go march - ing
in, Oh how I want to be there with them,
When the Saints go march - ing in.
D. C. al Fine

PREPARATORY EXERCISE FOR LITTLE BROWN JUG

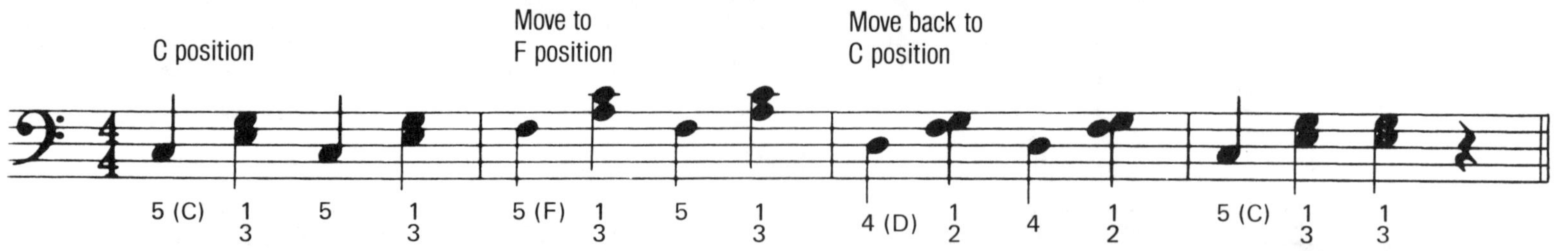

C position
Move to F position
Move back to C position
5 (C) 1 3 5 1 3
5 (F) 1 3 5 1 3
4 (D) 1 2 4 1 2
5 (C) 1 3 1 3

LITTLE BROWN JUG

MIDDLE
C
E F G A B C D E

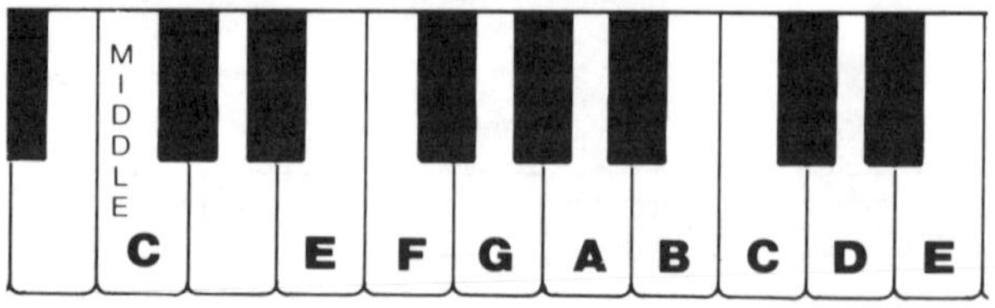

(8 NOTES FOR THE RIGHT HAND. E TO E)

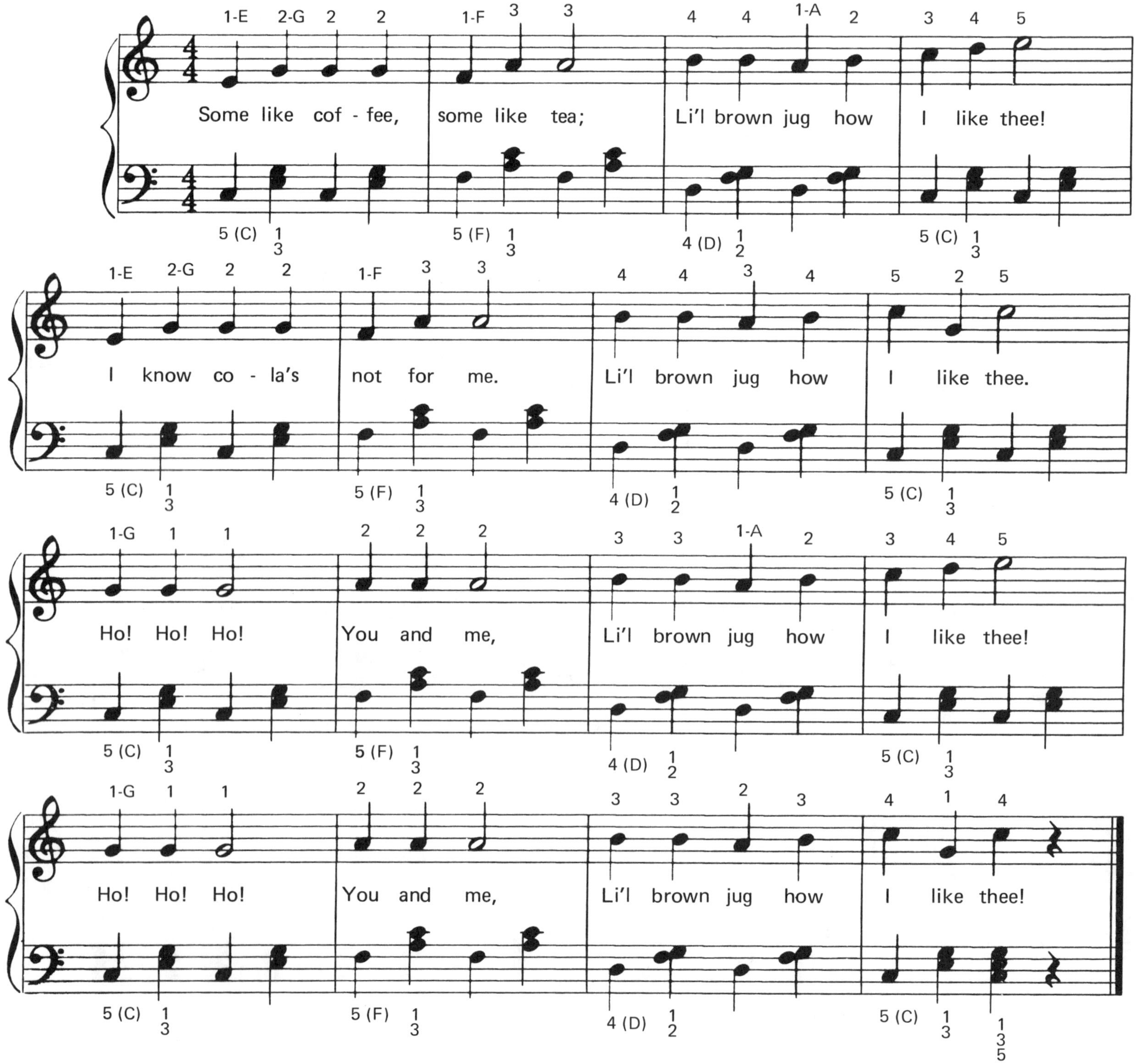

Some like cof - fee, some like tea; Li'l brown jug how I like thee!
I know co - la's not for me. Li'l brown jug how I like thee.
Ho! Ho! Ho! You and me, Li'l brown jug how I like thee!
Ho! Ho! Ho! You and me, Li'l brown jug how I like thee!
5 (C)
5 (F)
4 (D)
1-E 2-G 1-F 1-G 1-A

LOW
MIDDLE
B C D E F G A
C D E F G A

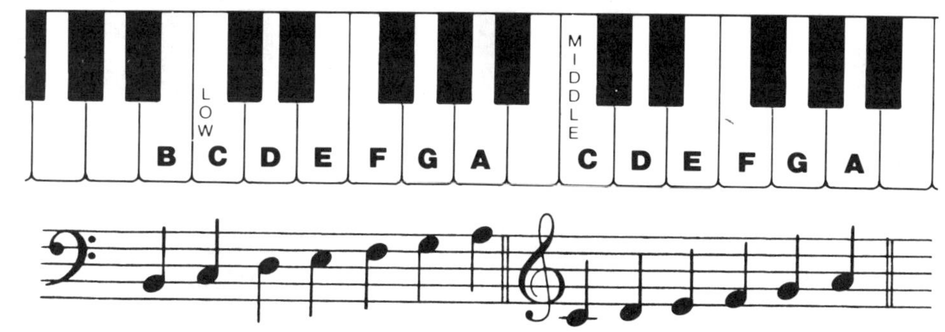

THIS OLD MAN

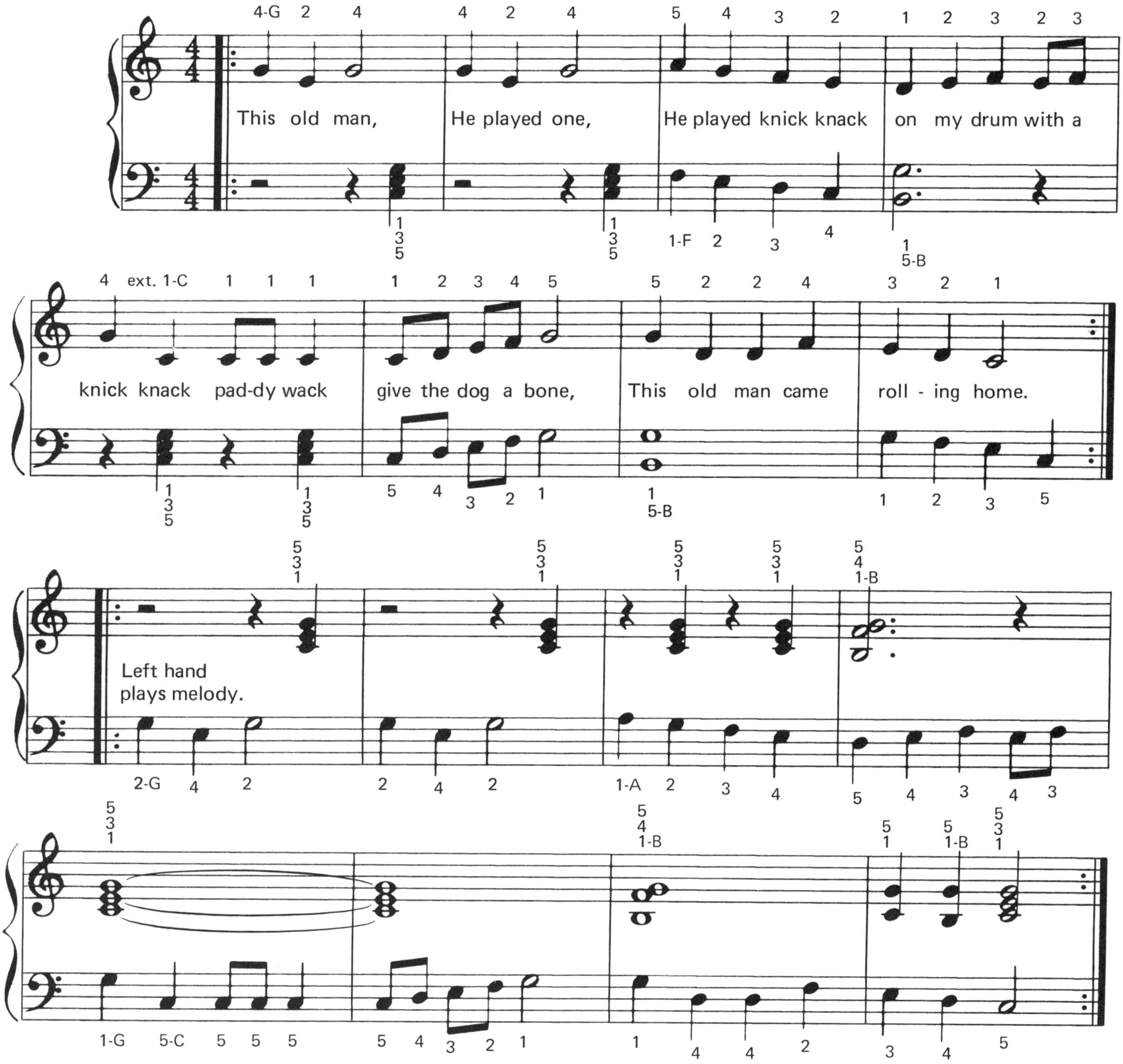

This old man,
He played one,
He played knick knack
on my drum with a
knick knack pad-dy wack
give the dog a bone,
This old man came
roll - ing home.
Left hand plays melody.

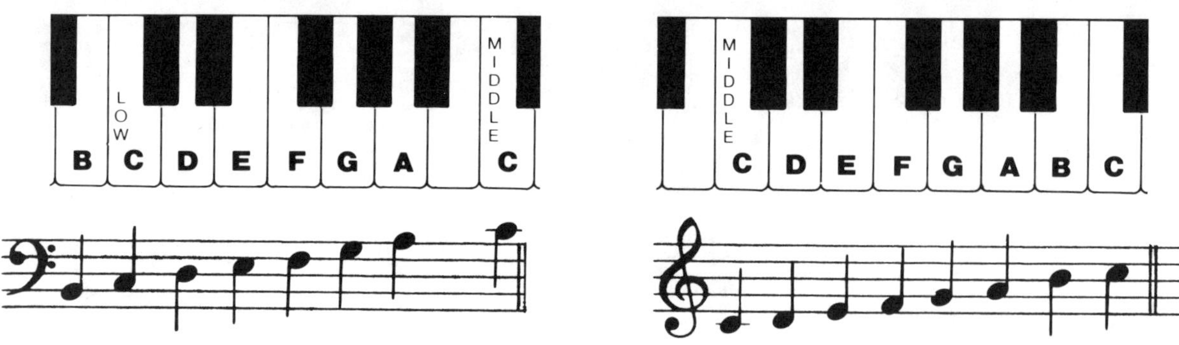

STARLIGHT WALTZ

(A TWO PAGE SONG.)

Fine

TO NEXT PAGE

ENHARMONIC TONES

F♯ and G♭ **D♯ and E♭** **C♯ and D♭** **G♯ and A♭** **A♯ and B♭**

Enharmonic means two different notations for the same tone.

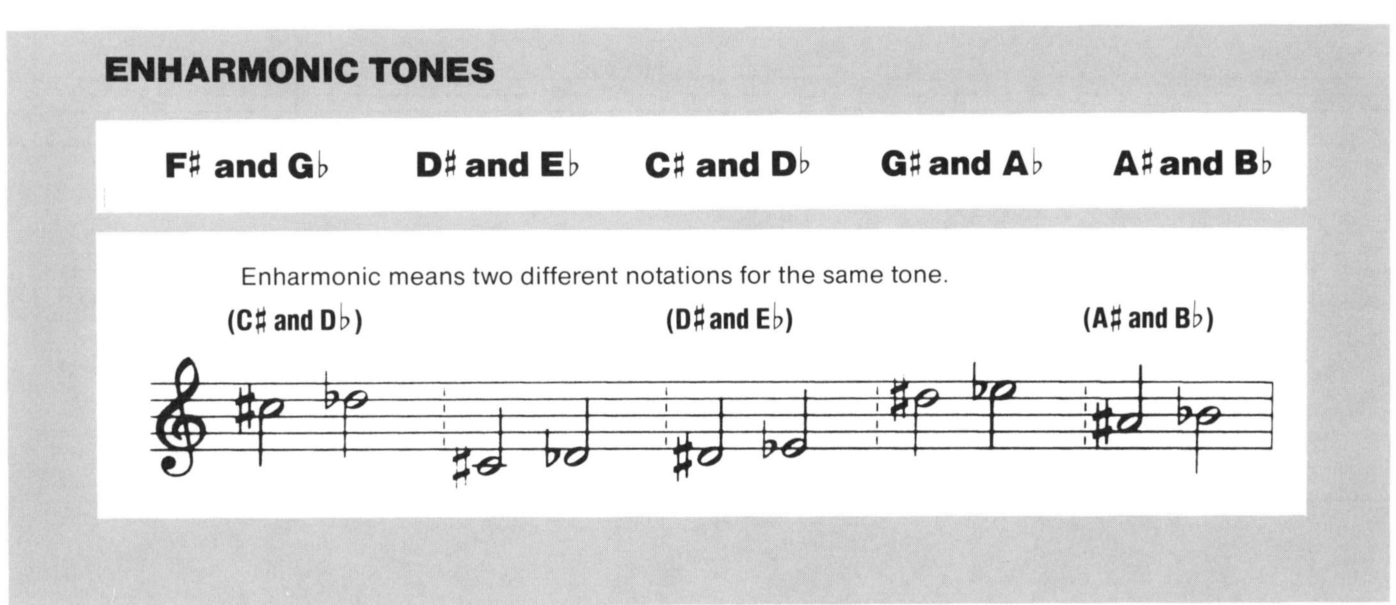

CHROMATIC SCALE (C)

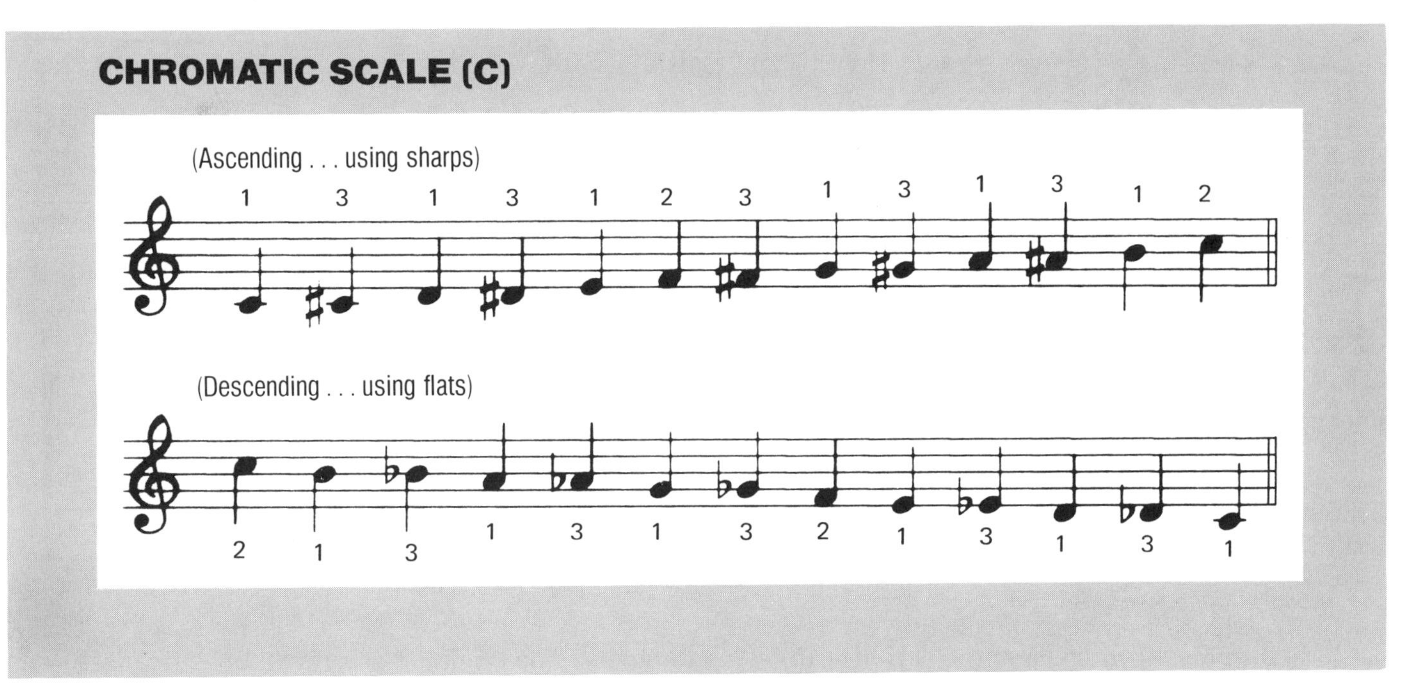

LOW
LOW
MIDDLE
F#
Bb
C#
F C E F A B C D
MIDDLE
C D E F G A
Bb

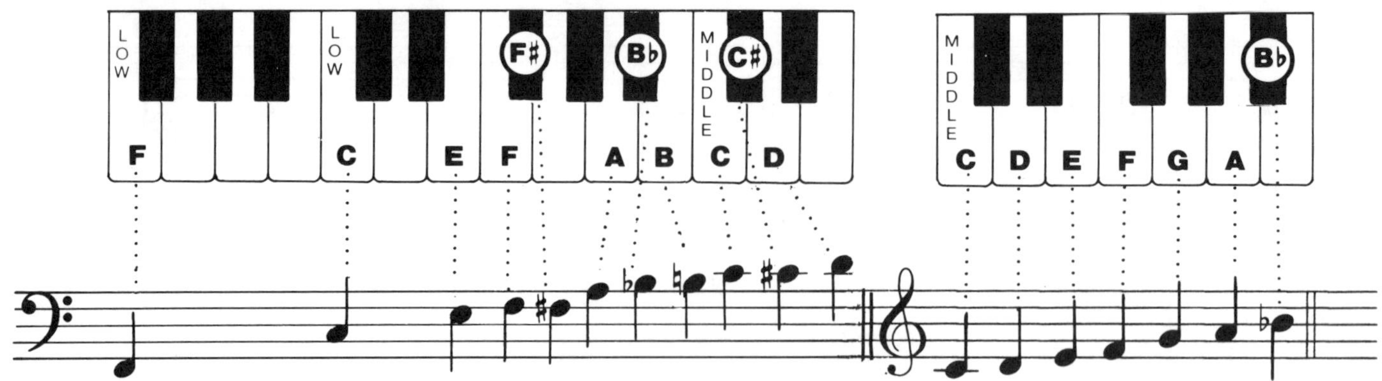

AURA LEE

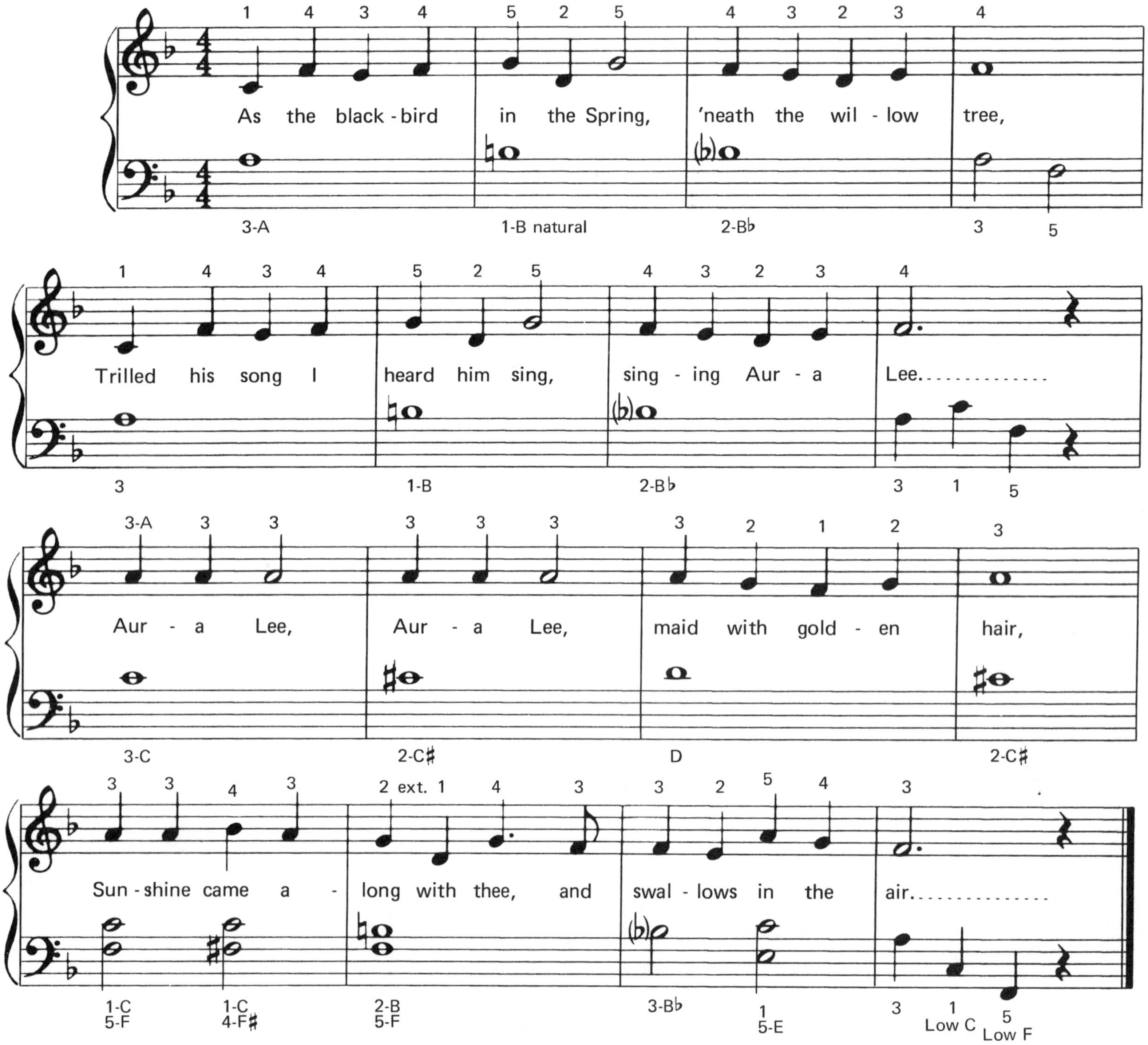

As the black - bird in the Spring, 'neath the wil - low tree,
3-A
1-B natural
2-Bb
Trilled his song I heard him sing, sing - ing Aur - a Lee.
1-B
2-Bb
Aur - a Lee, Aur - a Lee, maid with gold - en hair,
3-A
3-C
2-C#
D
2-C#
Sun - shine came a - long with thee, and swal - lows in the air.
2 ext. 1
1-C
5-F
1-C
4-F#
2-B
5-F
3-Bb
5-E
Low C
Low F

When a sharp, flat, or natural is shown in parenthesis (♯) (♭) (♮) it is a reminder. The reminder affects the specific measure.

SIGNATURE

Signature for the key of D

2 sharps . . F♯ and C♯

C♯
F♯
MIDDLE C
C♯
F♯
D E G A C A D E G A

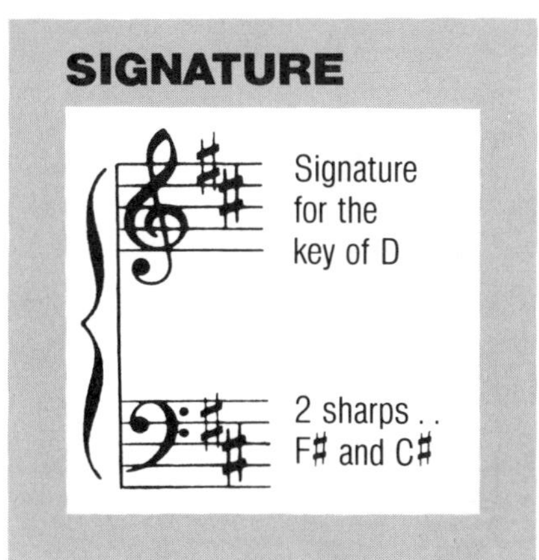

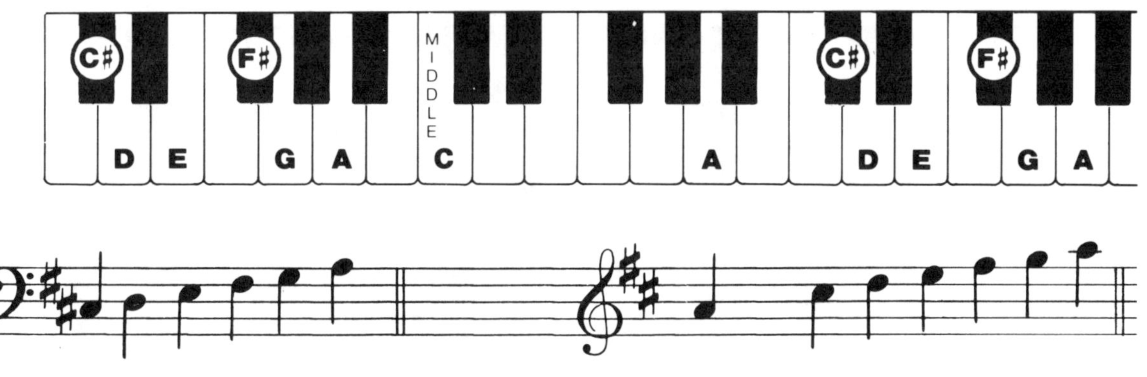

CLEMENTINE

(KEY OF D) (REMEMBER F♯ AND C♯)

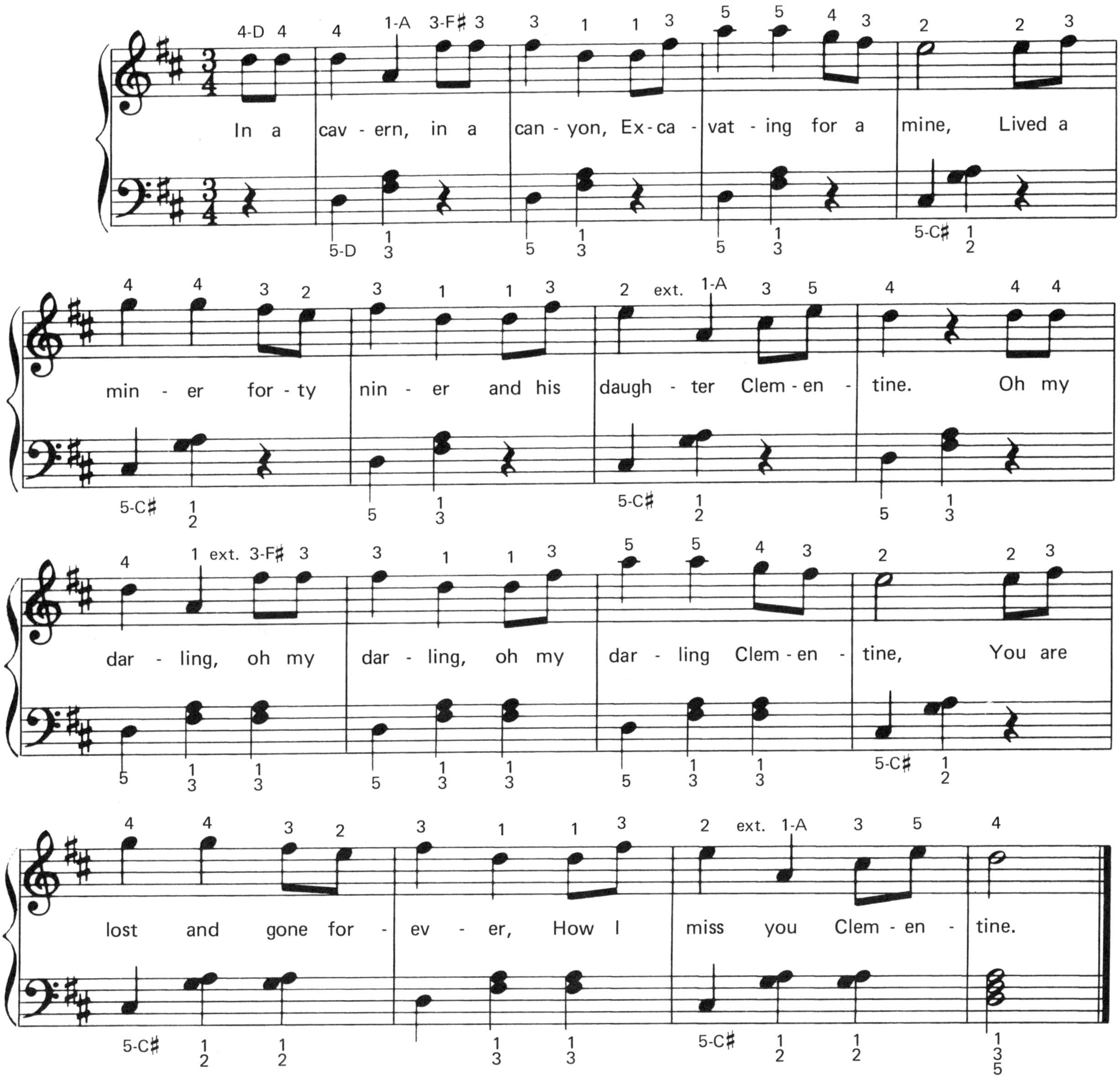

In a cav - ern, in a can - yon, Ex - ca - vat - ing for a mine, Lived a
min - er for - ty nin - er and his daugh - ter Clem - en - tine. Oh my
dar - ling, oh my dar - ling, oh my dar - ling Clem - en - tine, You are
lost and gone for - ev - er, How I miss you Clem - en - tine.

KEYBOARD CHART SHOWING ENHARMONIC NOTATION

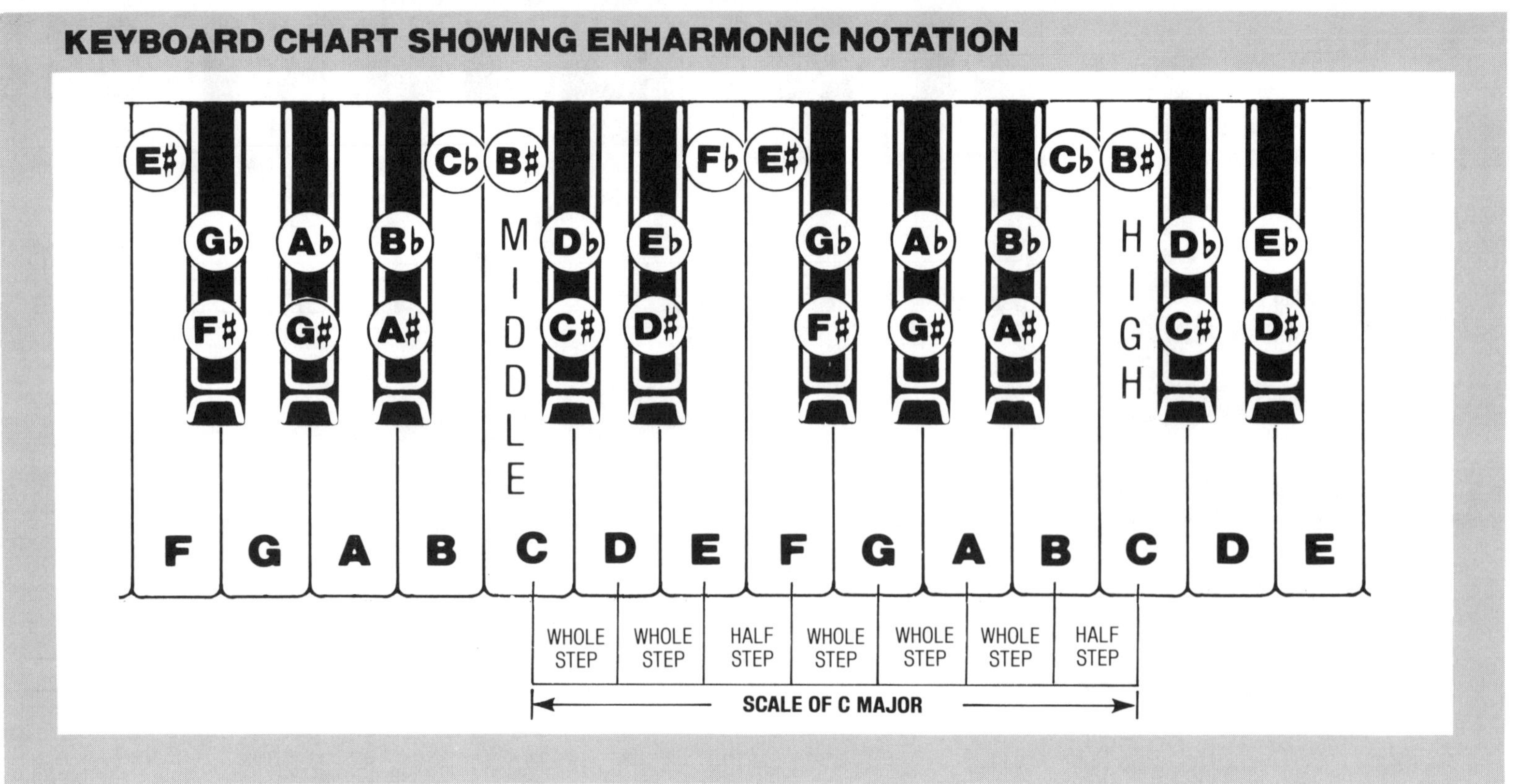

CHORD CONSTRUCTION

Chords are constructed by using certain intervals of the major scale. Any major scale is a succession of tones ascending or descending according to certain fixed intervals. A major scale is composed of two whole steps, a half step, three whole steps and a half step. Sharps (♯) or flats (♭) are not necessarily black keys. To raise any note one half step, play the first key to the right, whether it be black or white. To lower any note one half step, play the first key to the left, whether it be black or white.

CHORD INVERSIONS

Chords may be inverted and the notes will not appear in the 1, 3, 5 order. For example: C-E-G, E-G-C, G-C-E, are all C major chords. Changing the order of the notes will not change the chord name.

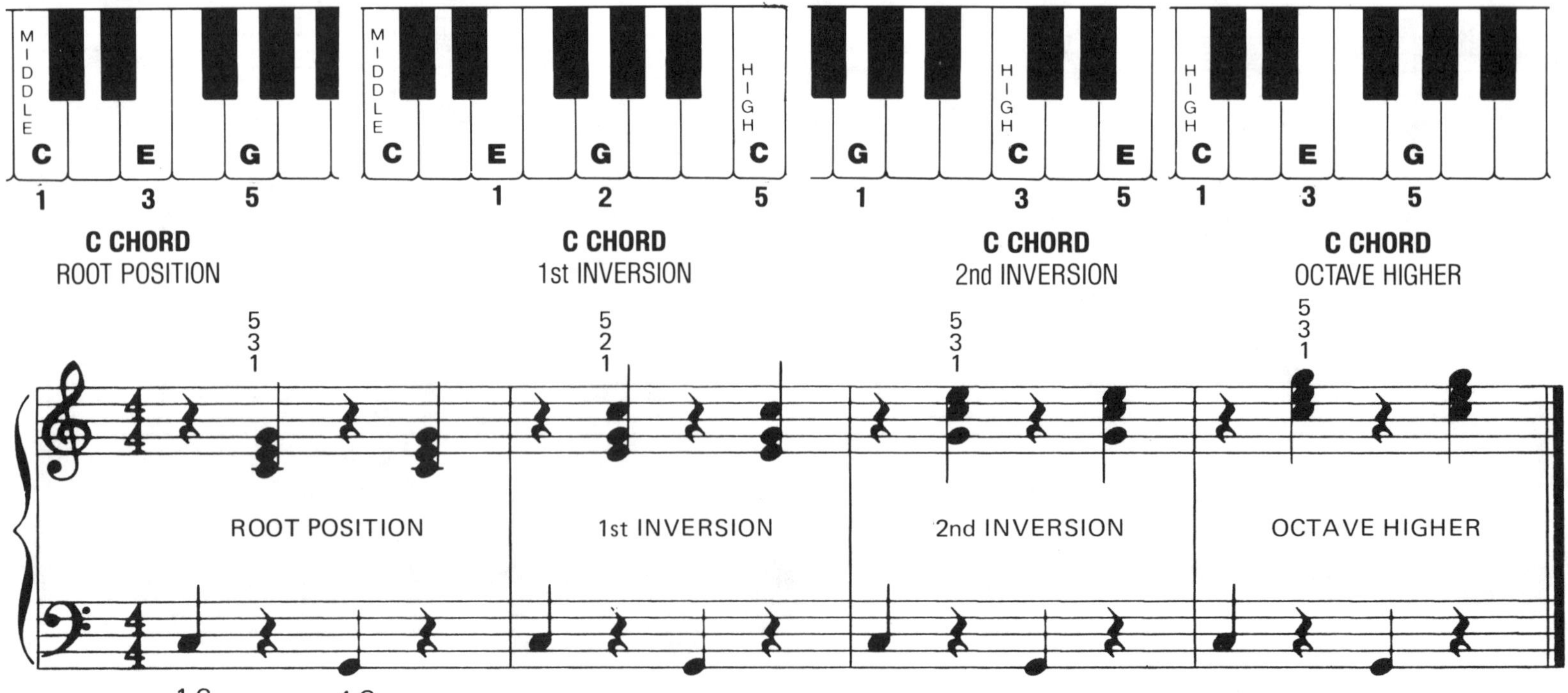

DOUBLE SHARP
Raises a note two half-steps. One half-step means the next key to the right . . . black or white.

CHORD CONSTRUCTION

The following examples are shown in the Key of C in order to indicate the use of any needed sharps or flats. Remember a double flat (♭♭) will lower any note two half steps. The double sharp (𝄪) will raise any note two half steps. Half steps may also be called half tones. Whole steps may also be called whole tones.

DOUBLE FLAT
Lowers a note two half-steps. One half-step means the next key to the left . . . black or white.

CHORD NAMES	NOTE NAMES	INTERVALS OF THE SCALE	USUALLY SHOWN
MAJOR	C — E — G	1 — 3 — 5	C
MINOR	C — E♭ — G	1 — ♭3 — 5	Cm
AUGMENTED	C — E — G♯	1 — 3 — ♯5	C aug. *or* C+
SEVENTH (dominant)	C — E — G — B♭	1 — 3 — 5 — ♭7	C7
MAJOR SEVENTH	C — E — G — B	1 — 3 — 5 — 7	C maj. 7
DIMINISHED SEVENTH	C — E♭ — G♭ — B♭♭ *(A)*	1 — ♭3 — ♭5 — ♭♭7	C dim. *or* C°
MAJOR NINTH	C — E — G — D	1 — 3 — 5 — 9	C maj. 9th
NINTH (dominant)	C — E — G — B♭ — D	1 — 3 — 5 — ♭7 — 9 *(5th sometimes omitted)*	C9
SIXTH	C — E — G — A	1 — 3 — 5 — 6	C6
MINOR SIXTH	C — E♭ — G — A	1 — ♭3 — 5 — 6	Cm6
AUGMENTED SEVENTH	C — E — G♯ — B♭	1 — 3 — ♯5 — ♭7	C+7

C CHORDS

All chords may be inverted. The Major Chord is shown with inversions to serve as an example.

C MAJOR (C) ROOT POSITION

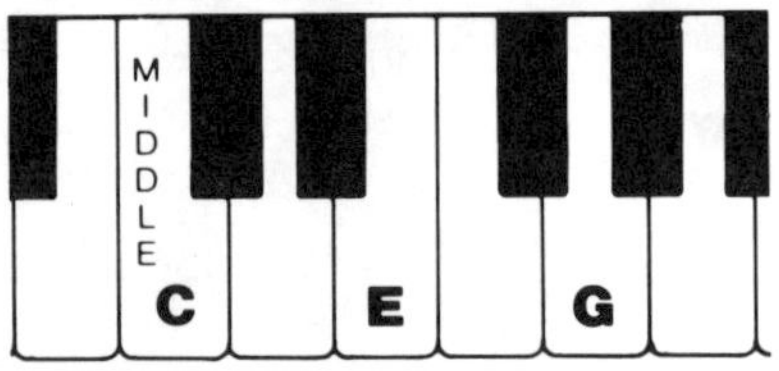

	C (MIDDLE C)	E	G
R.H.	1	3	5
L.H.	5	3	1

BASS: C or G

1ST INVERSION

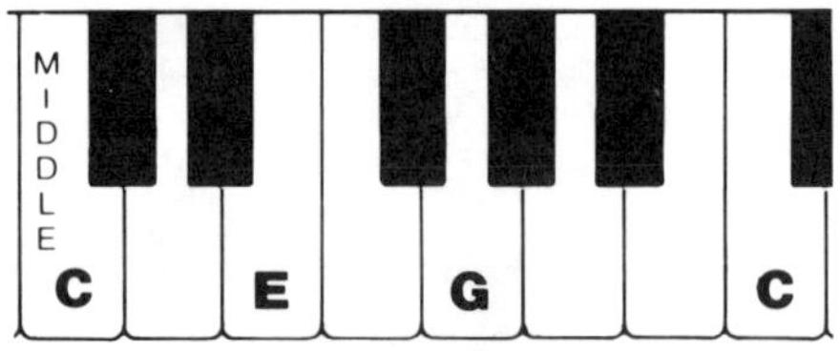

	E	G	C
R.H.	1	2	5
L.H.	5	3	1

BASS: C or G

2ND INVERSION

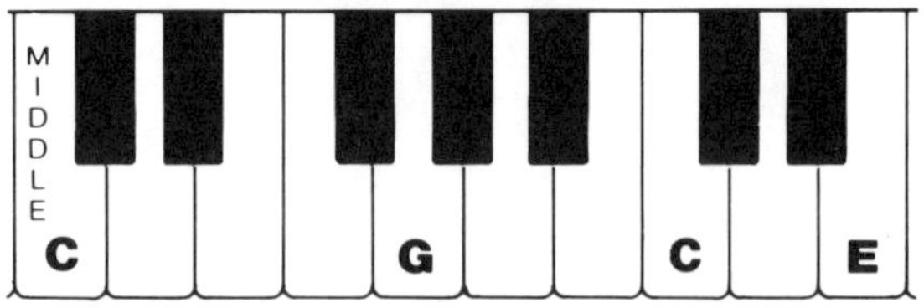

	G	C	E
R.H.	1	3	5
L.H.	5	2	1

BASS: C or G

C SIXTH (C6)

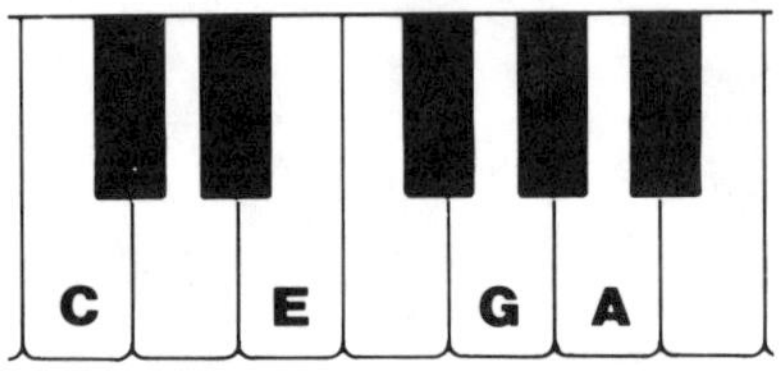

	C	E	G	A
R.H.	1	2	4	5
L.H.	5	3	2	1

BASS: C or G

C MAJOR SEVENTH (C maj 7)

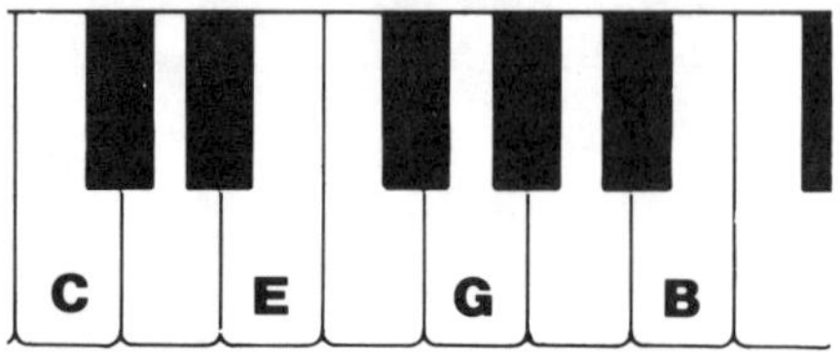

	C	E	G	B
R.H.	1	2	3	5
L.H.	5	3	2	1

BASS: C or G

C SEVENTH (C7)

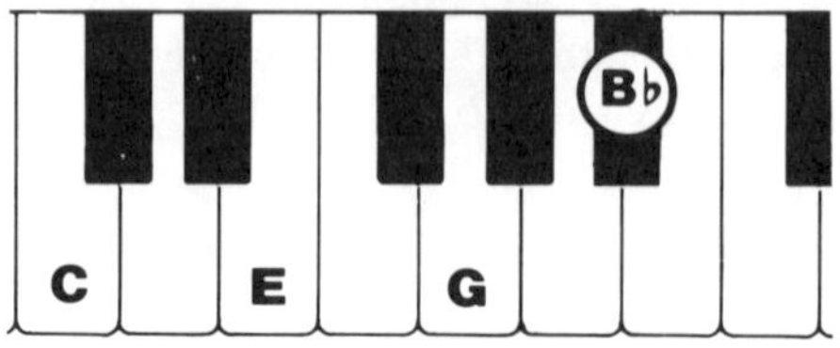

	C	E	G	B♭
R.H.	1	2	3	4
L.H.	5	3	2	1

BASS: C or G

C NINTH (C9)

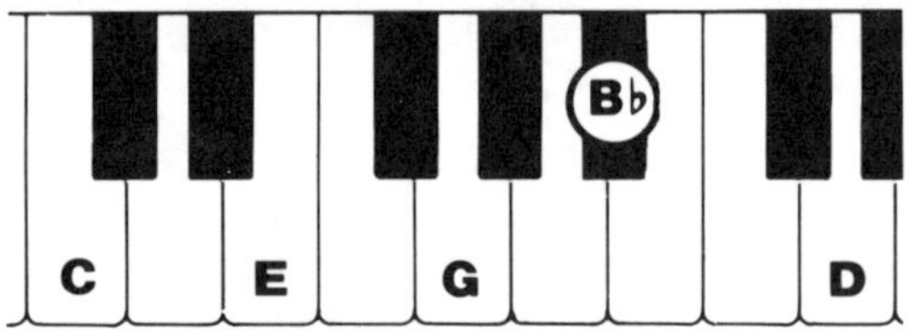

	C	E	G	B♭	D
R.H.	1	2	3	4	5
L.H.	5	4	3	2	1

BASS: C or G

C MAJOR NINTH (C maj 9)

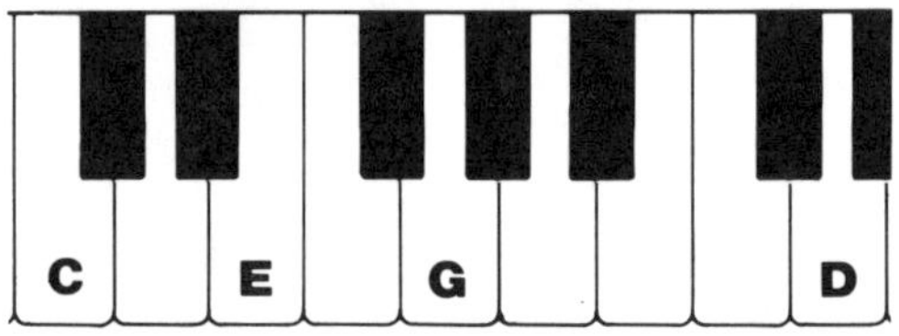

	C	E	G	D
R.H.	1	2	3	5
L.H.	5	3	2	1

BASS: C or G

C DIMINISHED (C°)

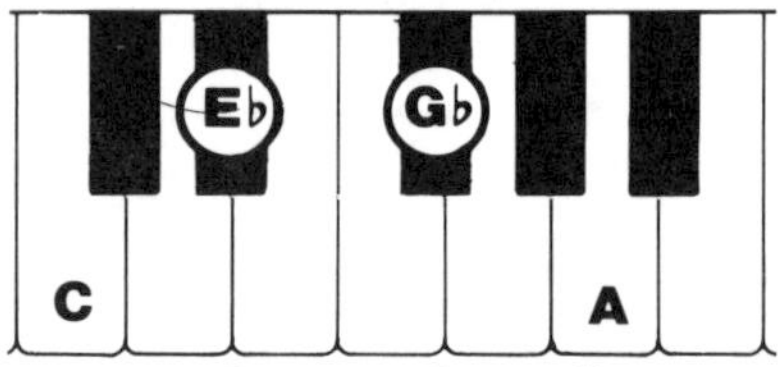

	C	E♭	G♭	A
R.H.	1	2	3	5
L.H.	5	3	2	1

BASS: C

C AUGMENTED (C+)

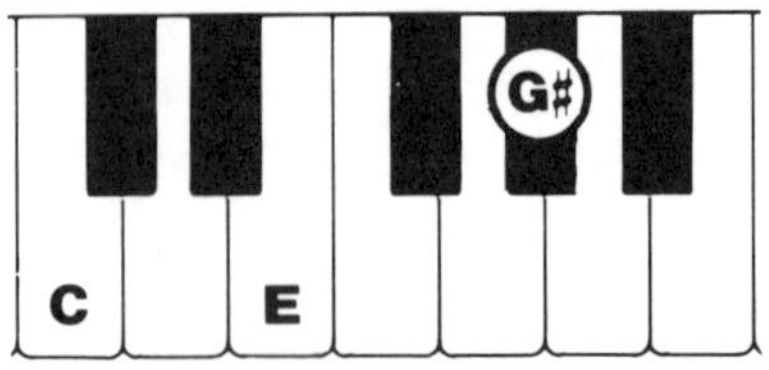

	C	E	G♯
R.H.	1	2	4
L.H.	5	3	1

BASS: C

C MINOR (Cm)

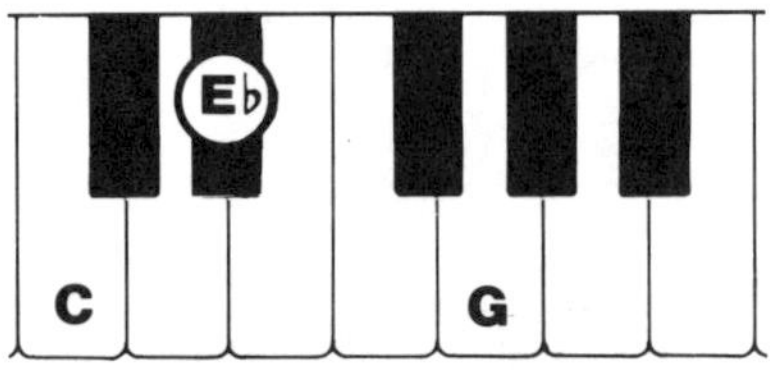

	C	E♭	G
R.H.	1	3	5
L.H.	5	3	1

BASS: C or G

C MINOR SIXTH (Cm6)

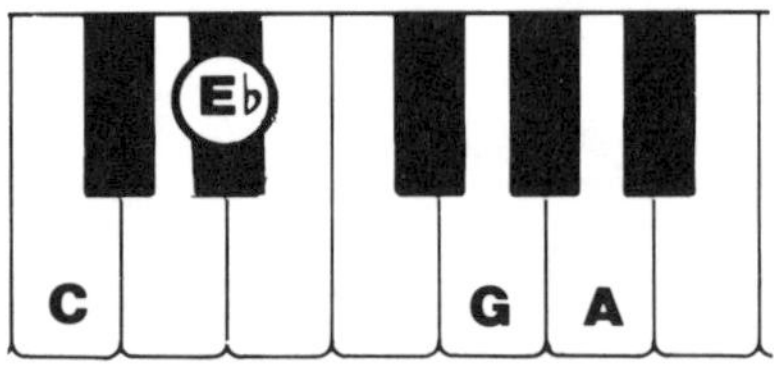

	C	E♭	G	A
R.H.	1	2	4	5
L.H.	5	3	2	1

BASS: C or G

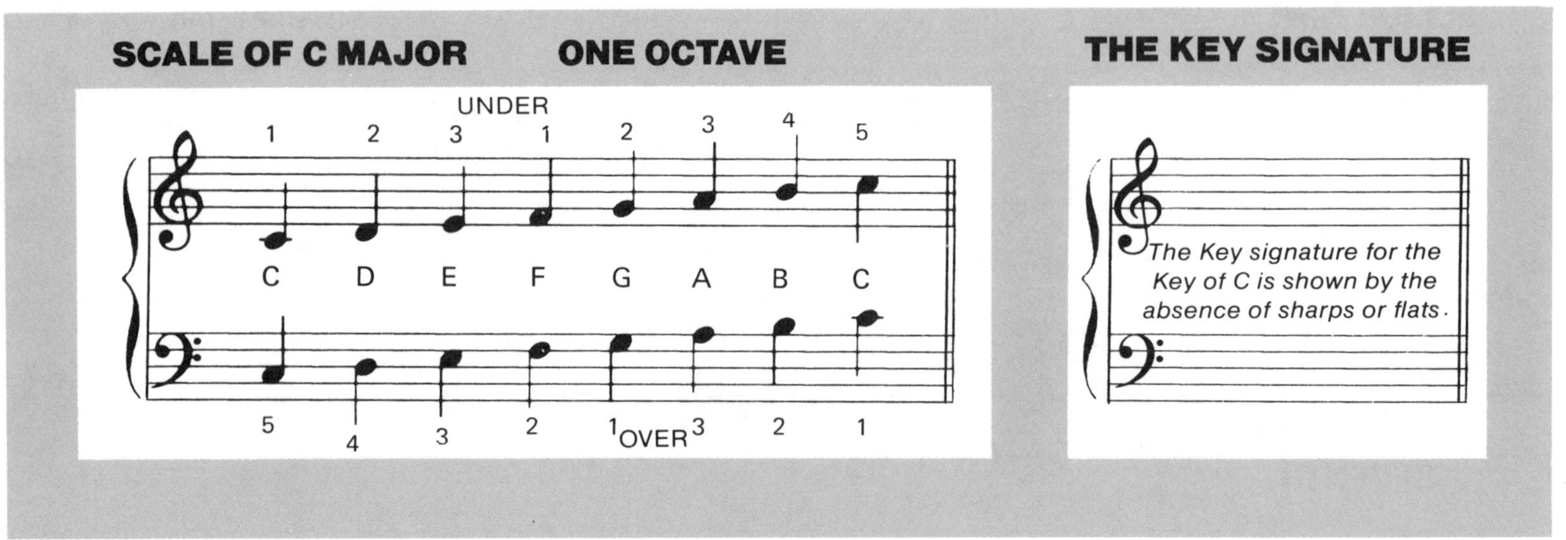

G CHORDS

All chords may be inverted. The Major Chord is shown with inversions to serve as an example.

G MAJOR (G) ROOT POSITION

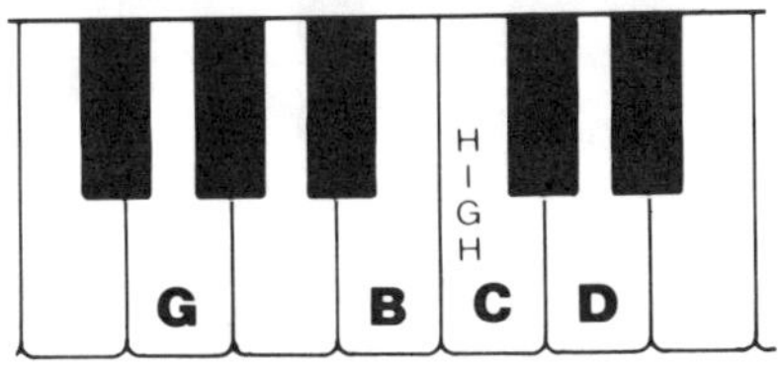

	G	B	HIGH C	D
R.H. →	1	3		5
L.H. →	5	3		1
BASS →	G or D			

1ST INVERSION OCTAVE LOWER

	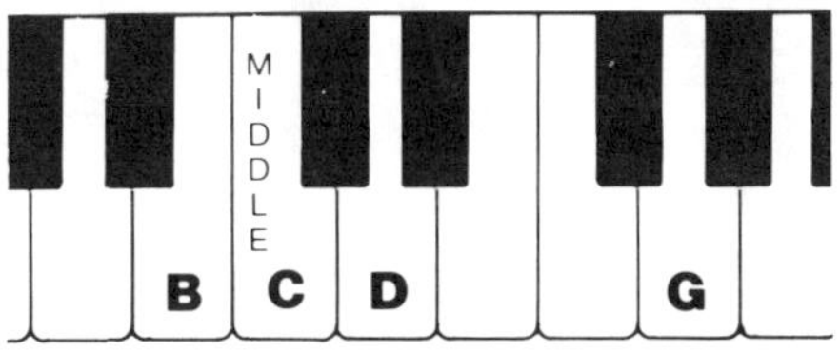 B	MIDDLE C	D	G
R.H. →	1		2	5
L.H. →	5		3	1
BASS →	G or D			

2ND INVERSION OCTAVE LOWER

	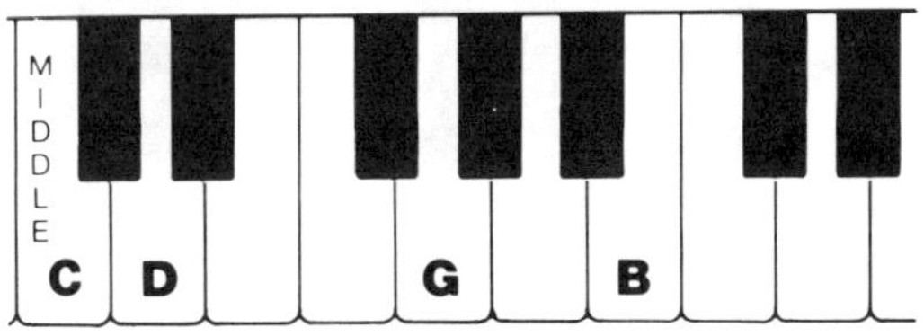 MIDDLE C	D	G	B
R.H. →		1	3	5
L.H. →		5	2	1
BASS →	G or D			

G SIXTH (G6)

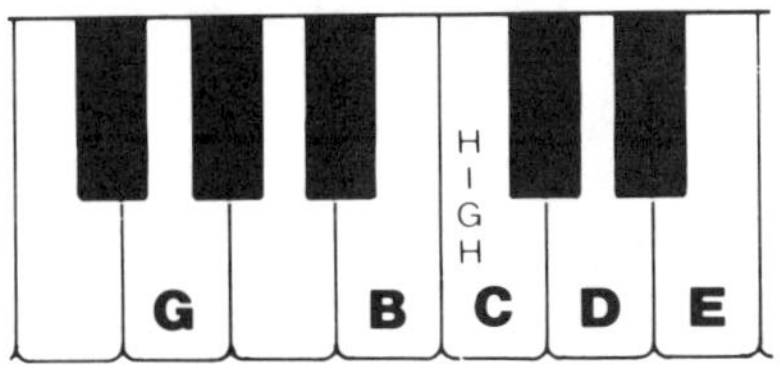

	G	B	HIGH C	D	E
R.H. →	1	2		4	5
L.H. →	5	3		2	1
BASS →	G or D				

G MAJOR SEVENTH (G maj 7)

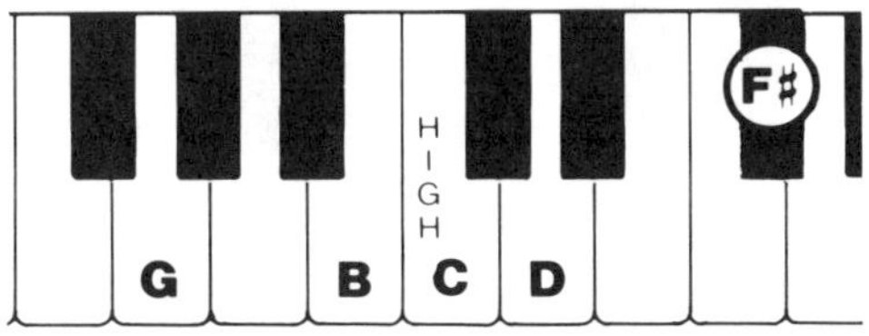

	G	B	HIGH C	D	F♯
R.H. →	1	2		3	5
L.H. →	5	3		2	1
BASS →	G or D				

G SEVENTH (G7)

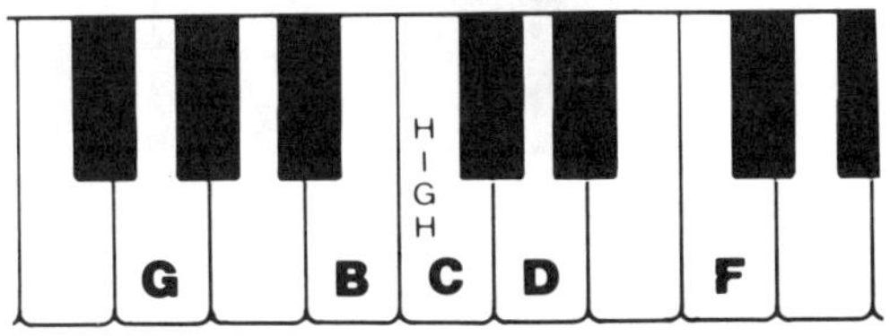

	G	B	HIGH C	D	F
R.H. →	1	2		3	5
L.H. →	5	3		2	1
BASS →	G or D				

G NINTH (G9)

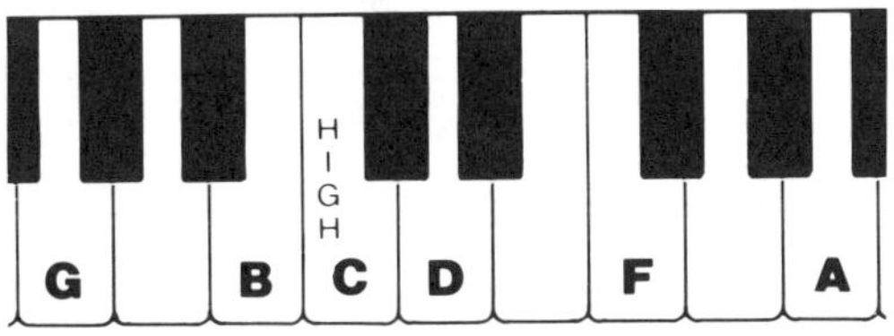

	G	B	HIGH C	D	F	A
R.H. →	1	2		3	4	5
L.H. →	5	4		3	2	1
BASS →	G or D					

G MAJOR NINTH (G maj 9)

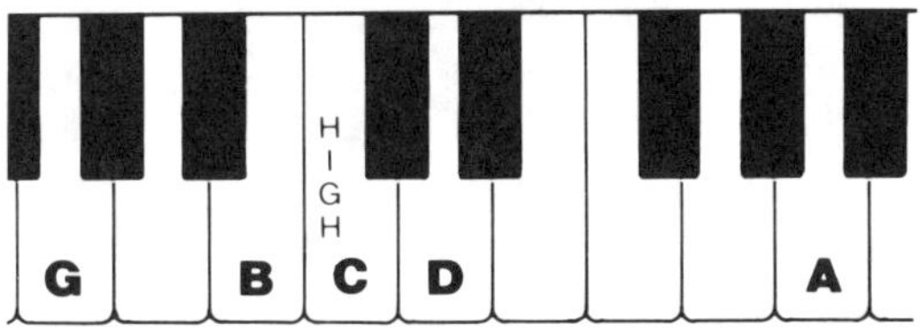

	G	B	HIGH C	D	A
R.H. →	1	2		3	5
L.H. →	5	3		2	1
BASS →	G or D				

G DIMINISHED (G°)

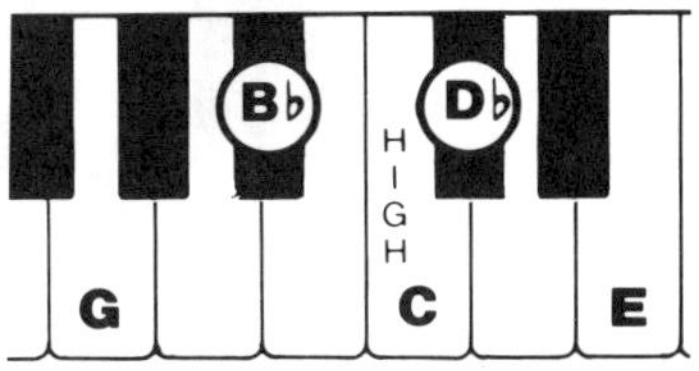

	G	B♭	HIGH C	D♭	E
R.H. →	1	2		3	5
L.H. →	5	3		2	1
BASS →	G				

G AUGMENTED (G+)

	G	B	HIGH C	D♯
R.H. →	1	2		4
L.H. →	5	3		1
BASS →	G			

G MINOR (Gm)

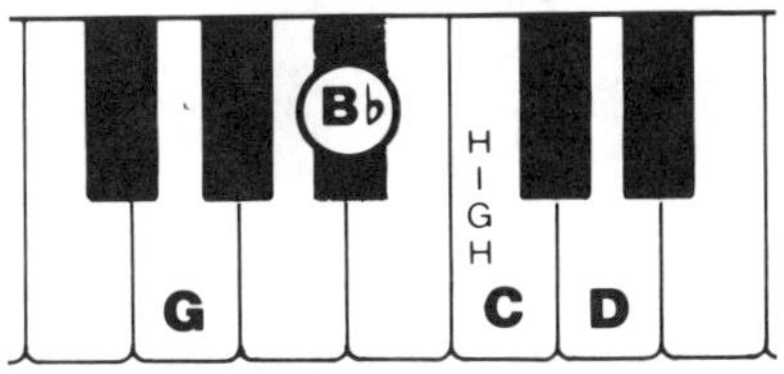

	G	B♭	HIGH C	D
R.H. →	1	3		5
L.H. →	5	3		1
BASS →	G or D			

G MINOR SIXTH (Gm6)

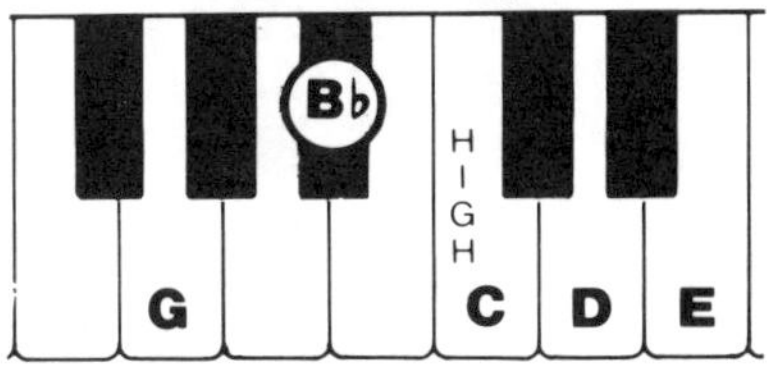

	G	B♭	HIGH C	D	E
R.H. →	1	2		4	5
L.H. →	5	3		2	1
BASS →	G or D				

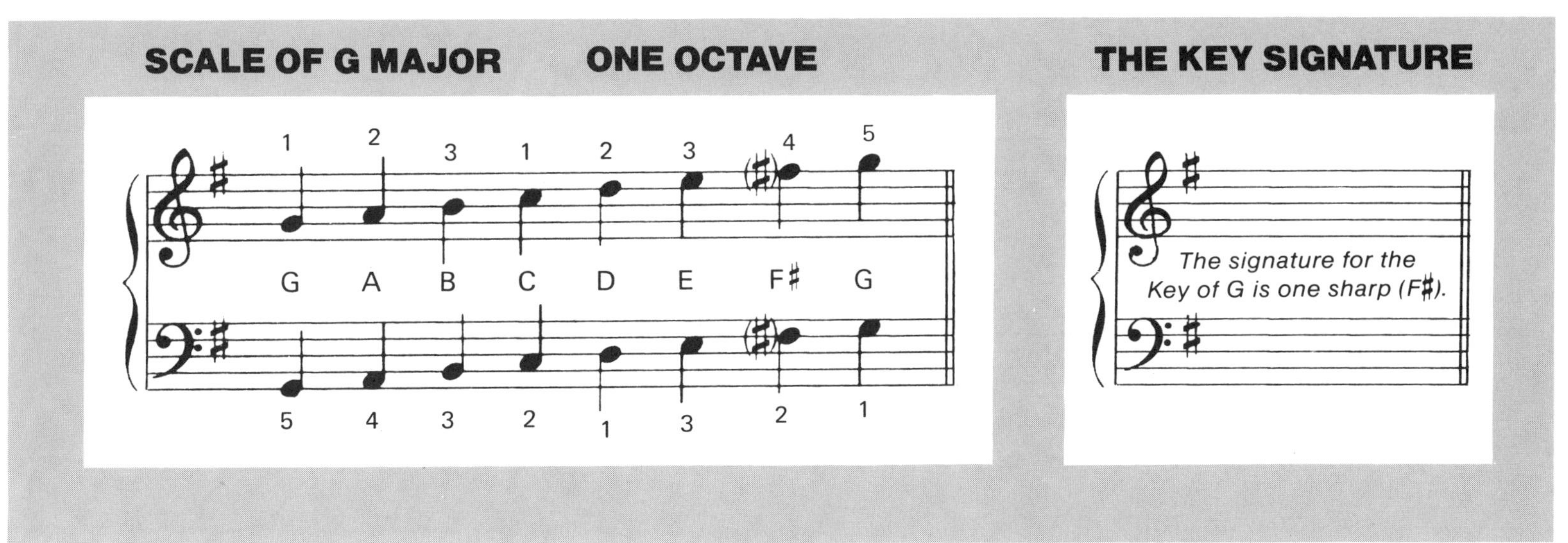

D CHORDS

All chords may be inverted. The Major Chord is shown with inversions to serve as an example.

D MAJOR (D) ROOT POSITION

Keys: C D F♯ A (MIDDLE C)

R.H. →	1	3	5
L.H. →	5	3	1
BASS →	D or A		

1ST INVERSION

Keys: C F♯ A D (MIDDLE C)

R.H. →	1	2	5
L.H. →	5	3	1
BASS →	D or A		

2ND INVERSION . . . OCTAVE LOWER

Keys: A C D F♯ (MIDDLE C)

R.H. →	1	3	5
L.H. →	5	2	1
BASS →	D or A		

D SIXTH (D6)

Keys: C D F♯ A B (MIDDLE C)

R.H. →	1	2	4	5
L.H. →	5	3	2	1
BASS →	D or A			

D MAJOR SEVENTH (D maj 7)

Keys: C D F♯ A C♯ (MIDDLE C)

R.H. →	1	2	3	5
L.H. →	5	3	2	1
BASS →	D or A			

D SEVENTH (D7)

Keys: C D F♯ A C (MIDDLE C)

R.H. →	1	2	3	5
L.H. →	5	3	2	1
BASS →	D or A			

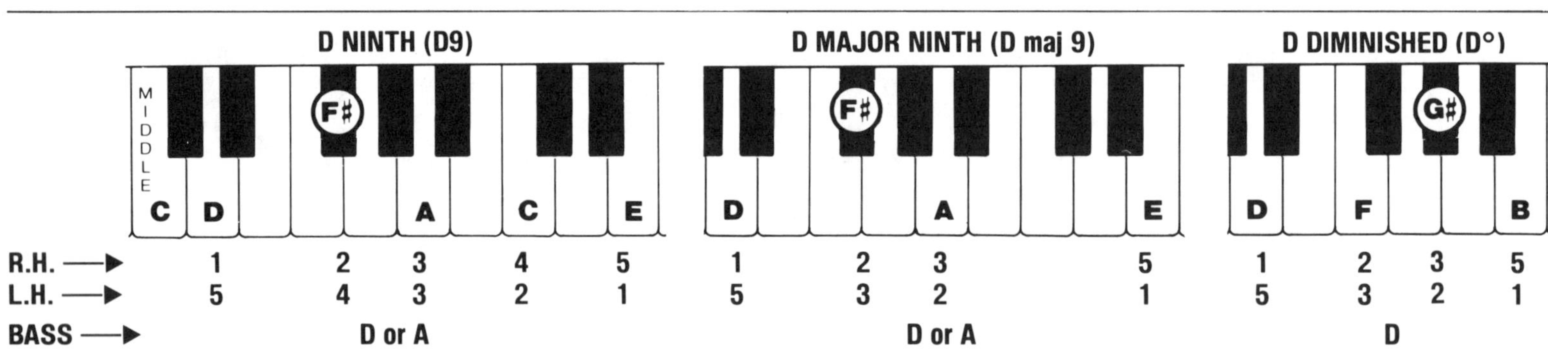

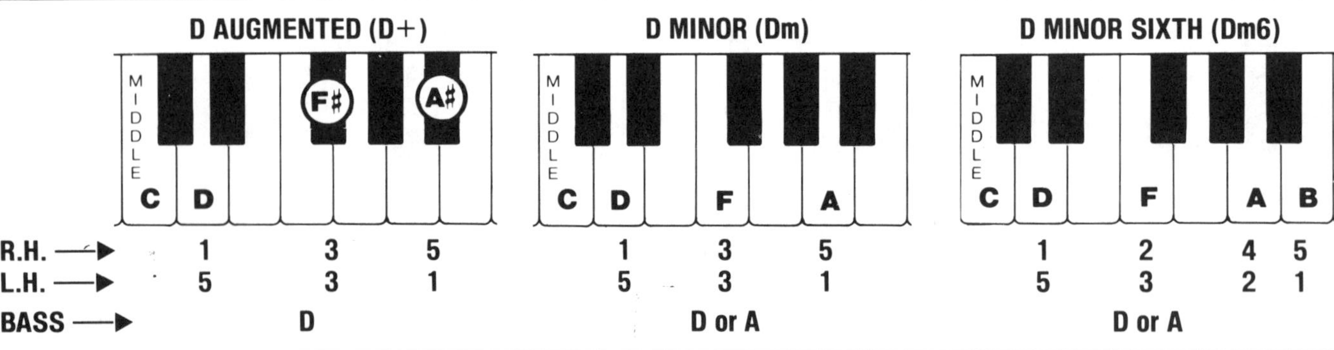

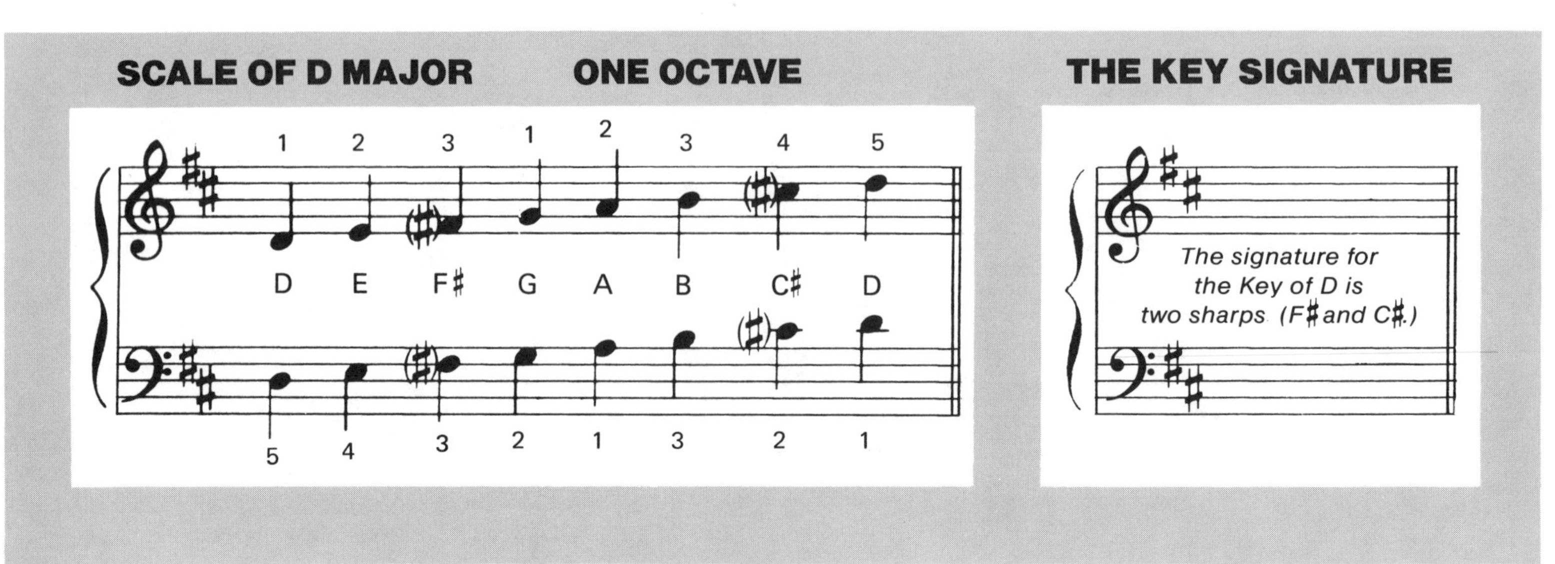

A CHORDS

All chords may be inverted. The Major Chord is shown with inversions to serve as an example.

A MAJOR (A) ROOT POSITION

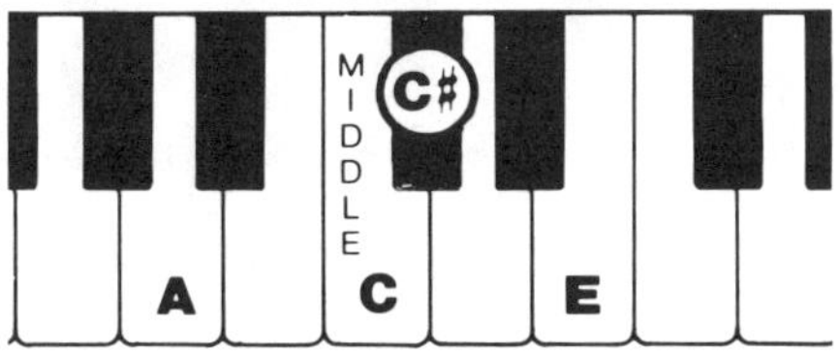

MIDDLE
C♯
A
C
E

R.H. ⟶ 1 3 5
L.H. ⟶ 5 3 1
BASS ⟶ A or E

1ST INVERSION

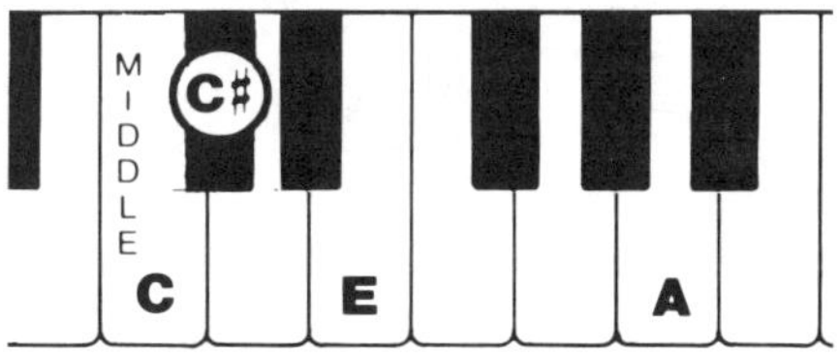

MIDDLE
C♯
C
E
A

R.H. ⟶ 1 2 5
L.H. ⟶ 5 3 1
BASS ⟶ A or E

2ND INVERSION

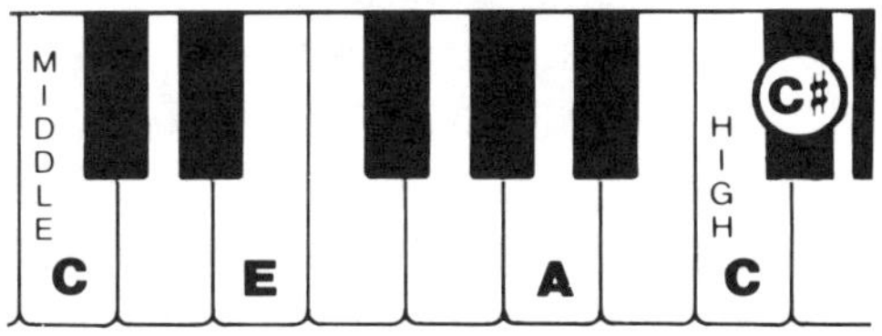

MIDDLE
HIGH
C♯
C
E
A
C

R.H. ⟶ 1 3 5
L.H. ⟶ 5 2 1
BASS ⟶ A or E

A SIXTH (A6)

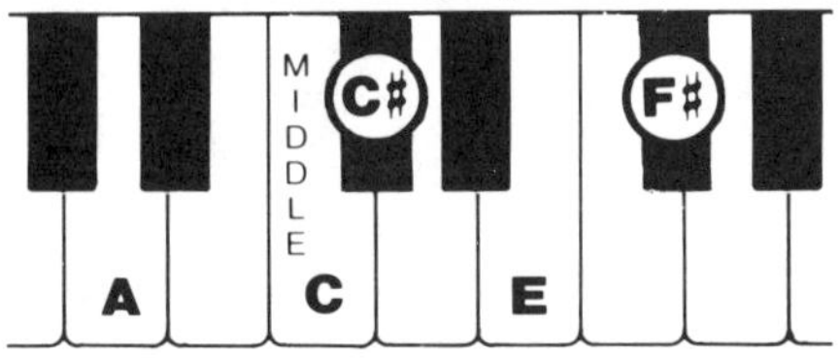

MIDDLE
C♯
F♯
A
C
E

R.H. ⟶ 1 2 3 4
L.H. ⟶ 5 3 2 1
BASS ⟶ A or E

A MAJOR SEVENTH (A maj 7)

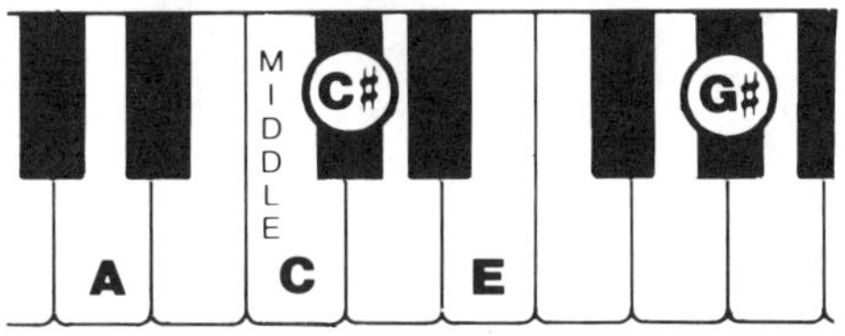

MIDDLE
C♯
G♯
A
C
E

R.H. ⟶ 1 2 3 5
L.H. ⟶ 5 3 2 1
BASS ⟶ A or E

A SEVENTH (A7)

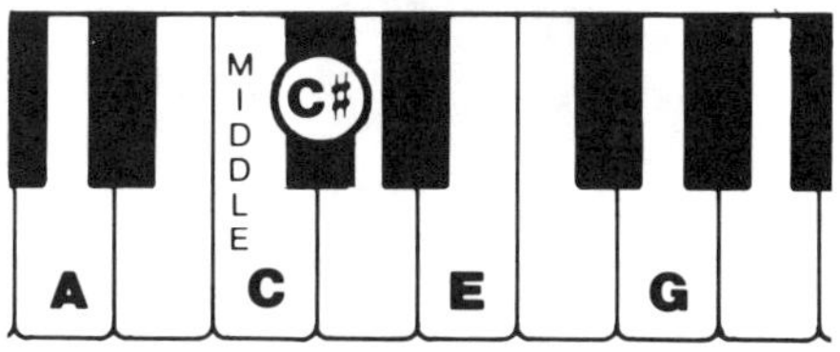

MIDDLE
C♯
A
C
E
G

R.H. ⟶ 1 2 3 5
L.H. ⟶ 5 3 2 1
BASS ⟶ A or E

A NINTH (A9)

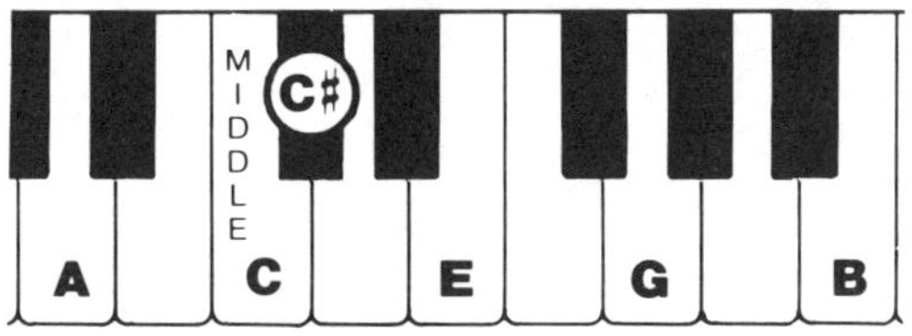

MIDDLE
C♯
A
C
E
G
B

R.H. ⟶ 1 2 3 4 5
L.H. ⟶ 5 4 3 2 1
BASS ⟶ A or E

A MAJOR NINTH (A maj 9)

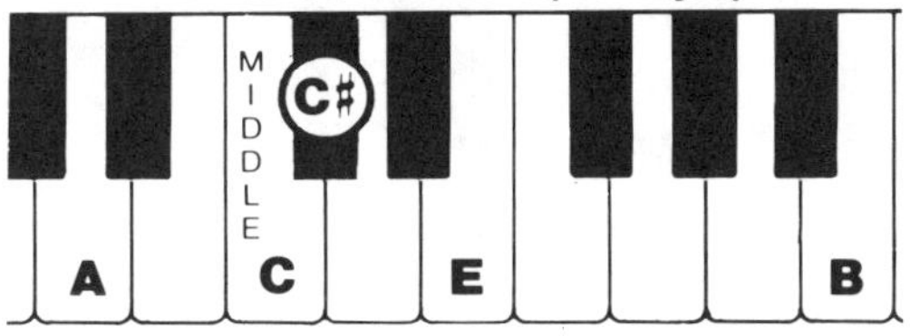

MIDDLE
C♯
A
C
E
B

R.H. ⟶ 1 2 3 5
L.H. ⟶ 5 3 2 1
BASS ⟶ A or E

A DIMINISHED (A°)

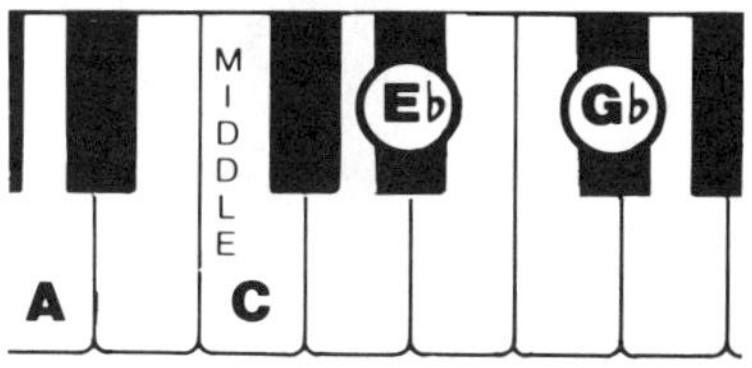

MIDDLE
E♭
G♭
A
C

R.H. ⟶ 1 2 3 5
L.H. ⟶ 5 3 2 1
BASS ⟶ A

A AUGMENTED (A+)

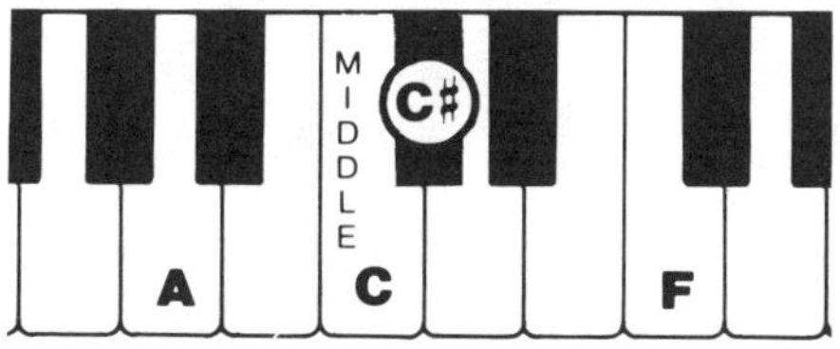

MIDDLE
C♯
A
C
F

R.H. ⟶ 1 3 5
L.H. ⟶ 5 3 1
BASS ⟶ A

A MINOR (Am)

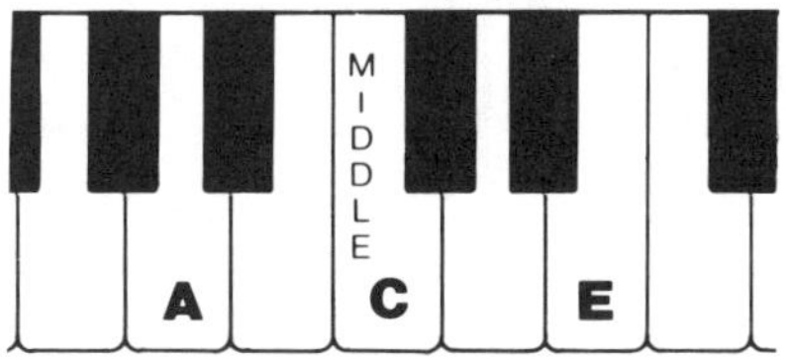

MIDDLE
A
C
E

R.H. ⟶ 1 3 5
L.H. ⟶ 5 3 1
BASS ⟶ A or E

MINOR SIXTH (Am6)

MIDDLE
F♯
A
C
E

R.H. ⟶ 1 2 4 5
L.H. ⟶ 5 3 2 1
BASS ⟶ A or E

SCALE OF A MAJOR ONE OCTAVE

1 2 3 1 2 3 4 5
A B C♯ D E F♯ G♯ A
5 4 3 2 1 3 2 1

THE KEY SIGNATURE

The signature for the Key of A is three sharps. (F♯, C♯, G♯.)

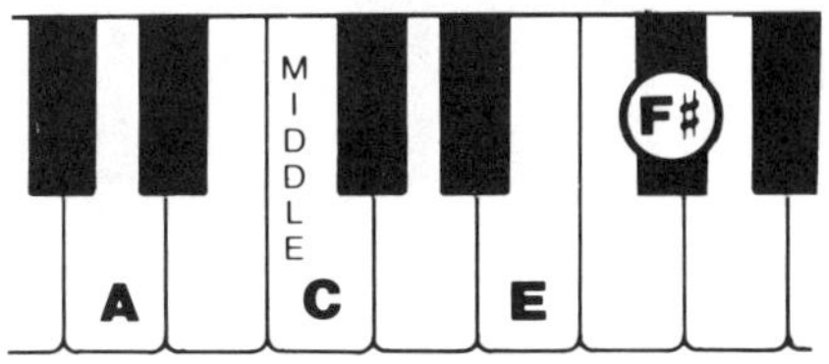

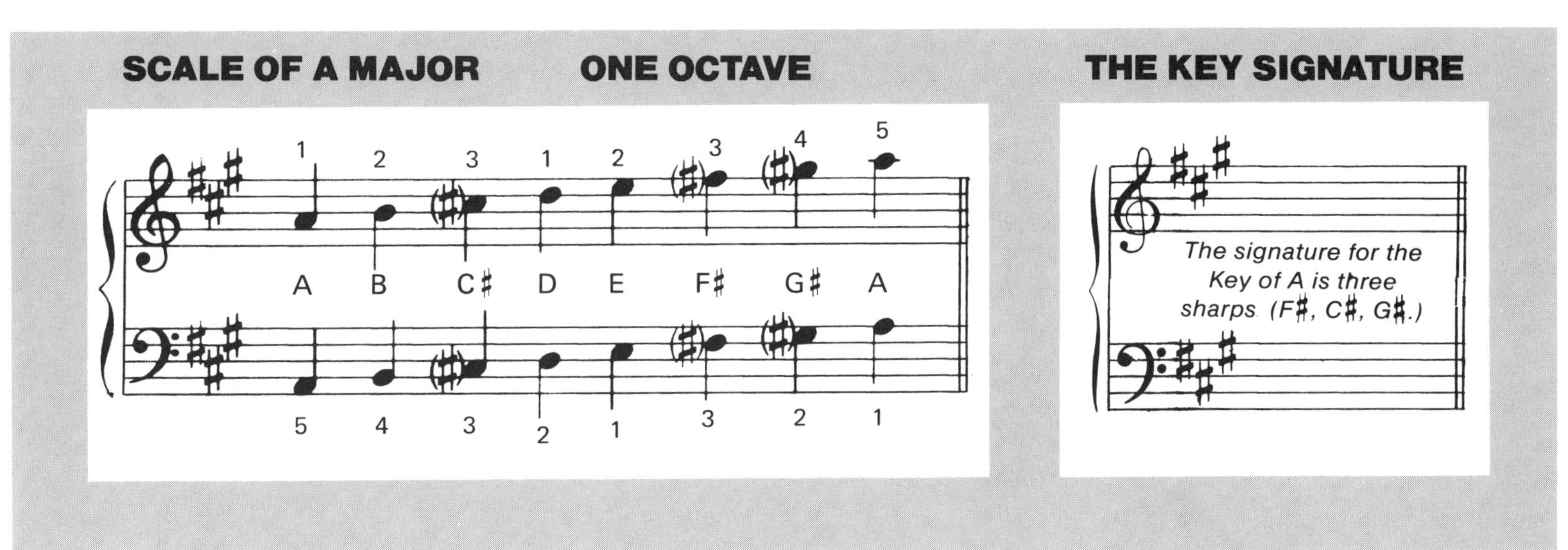

E CHORDS

All chords may be inverted. The Major Chord is shown with inversions to serve as an example.

E MAJOR (E) ROOT POSITION

MIDDLE C — E, G♯, B

R.H. ▶ 1 3 5
L.H. ▶ 5 3 1
BASS ▶ E or B

1ST INVERSION

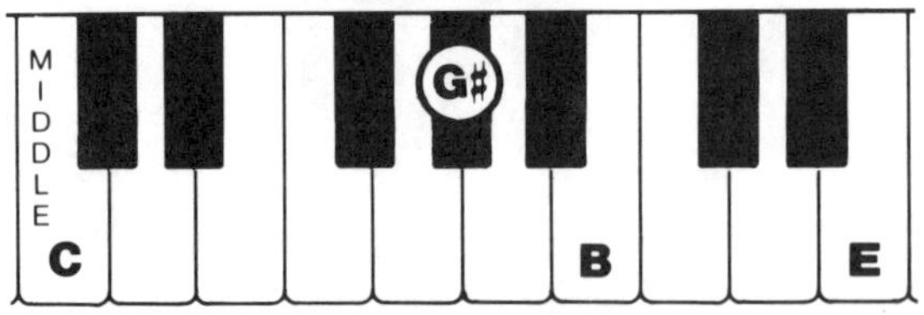

MIDDLE C — G♯, B, E

R.H. ▶ 1 2 5
L.H. ▶ 5 3 1
BASS ▶ E or B

2ND INVERSION . . . OCTAVE LOWER

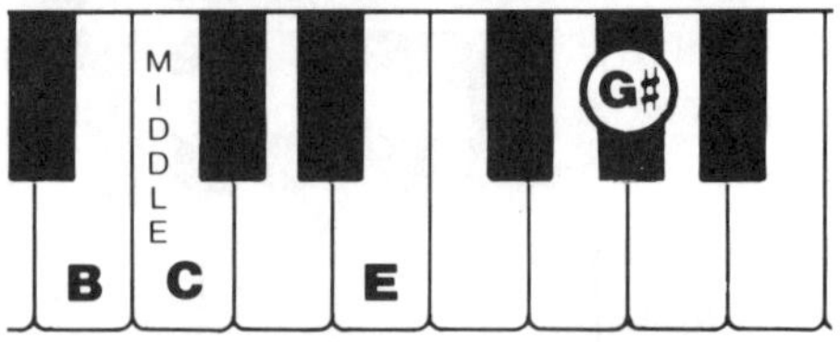

B, MIDDLE C — E, G♯

R.H. ▶ 1 3 5
L.H. ▶ 5 2 1
BASS ▶ E or B

E SIXTH (E6)

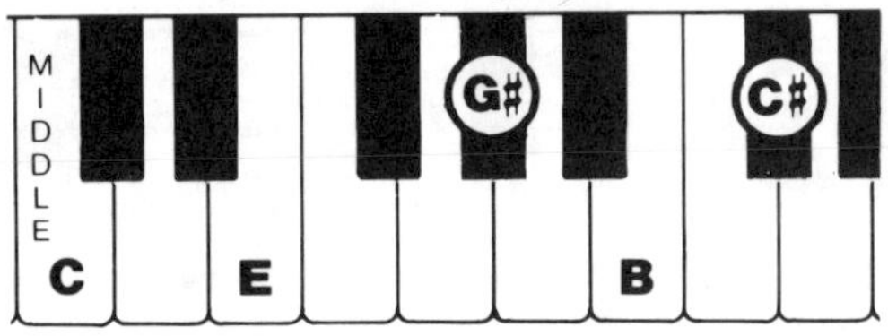

MIDDLE C — E, G♯, B, C♯

R.H. ▶ 1 2 3 4
L.H. ▶ 5 3 2 1
BASS ▶ E or B

E MAJOR SEVENTH (E maj 7)

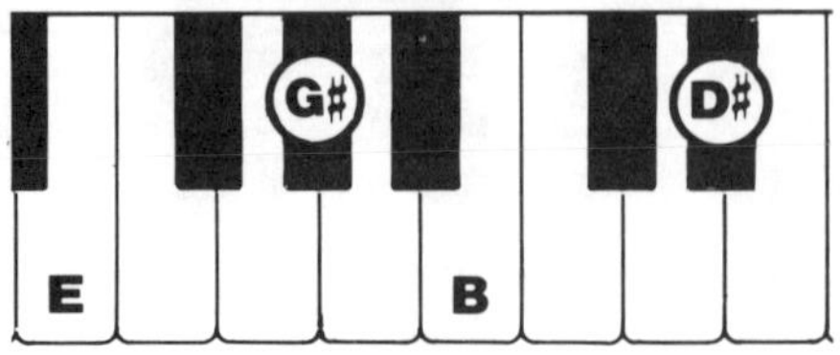

E, G♯, B, D♯

R.H. ▶ 1 2 3 5
L.H. ▶ 5 3 2 1
BASS ▶ E or B

E SEVENTH (E7)

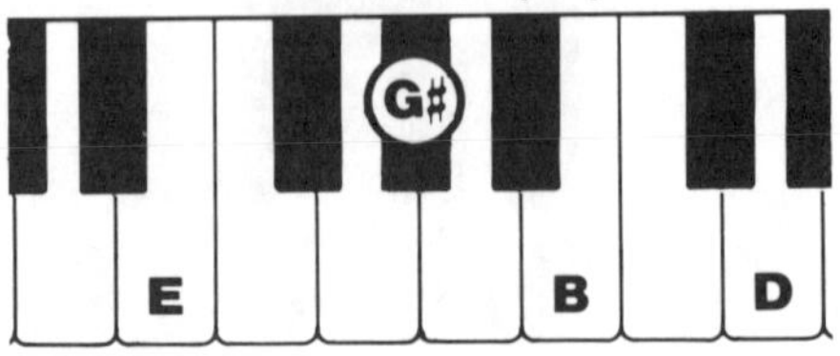

E, G♯, B, D

R.H. ▶ 1 2 3 5
L.H. ▶ 5 3 2 1
BASS ▶ E or B

E NINTH (E9)

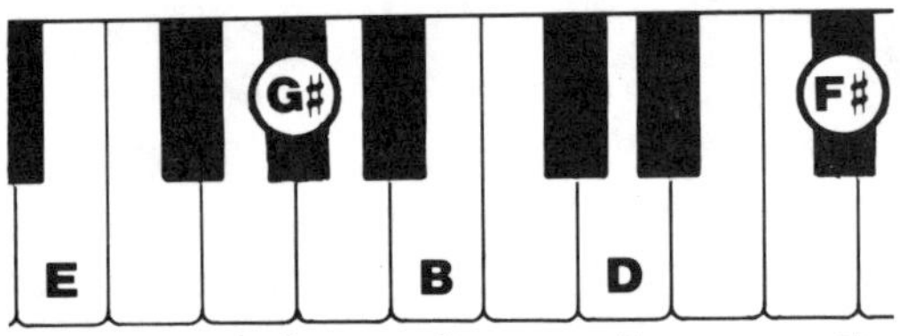

E, G♯, B, D, F♯

R.H. ▶ 1 2 3 4 5
L.H. ▶ 5 4 3 2 1
BASS ▶ E or B

E MAJOR NINTH (E maj 9)

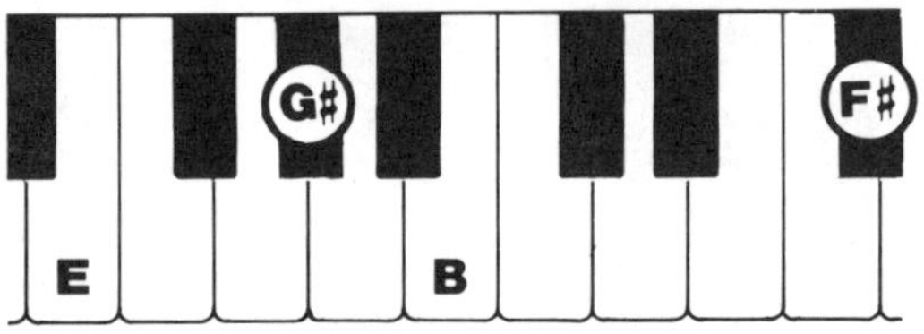

E, G♯, B, F♯

R.H. ▶ 1 2 3 5
L.H. ▶ 5 3 2 1
BASS ▶ E or B

E DIMINISHED (E°)

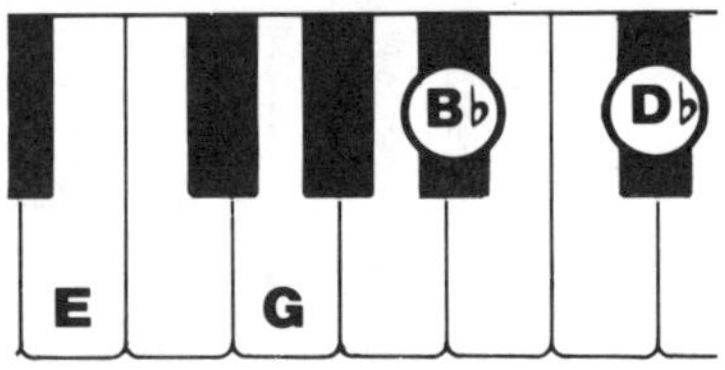

E, G, B♭, D♭

R.H. ▶ 1 2 3 5
L.H. ▶ 5 3 2 1
BASS ▶ E

E AUGMENTED (E+)

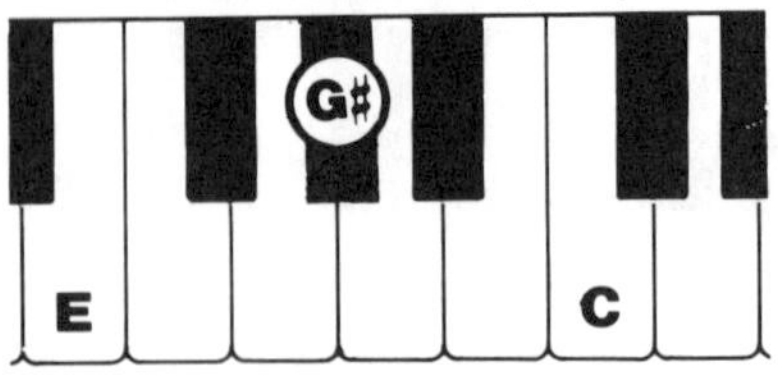

E, G♯, C

R.H. ▶ 1 3 5
L.H. ▶ 5 3 1
BASS ▶ E

E MINOR (Em)

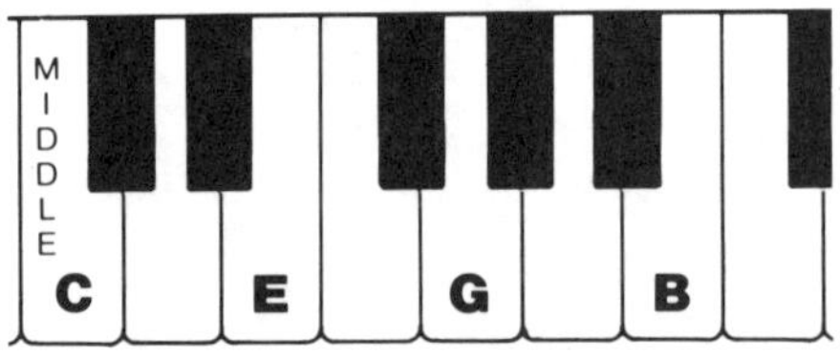

MIDDLE C — E, G, B

R.H. ▶ 1 3 5
L.H. ▶ 5 3 1
BASS ▶ E or B

E MINOR SIXTH (Em6)

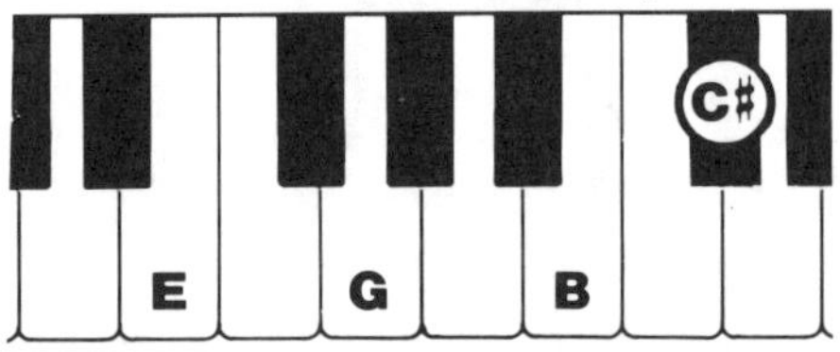

E, G, B, C♯

R.H. ▶ 1 2 4 5
L.H. ▶ 5 3 2 1
BASS ▶ E or B

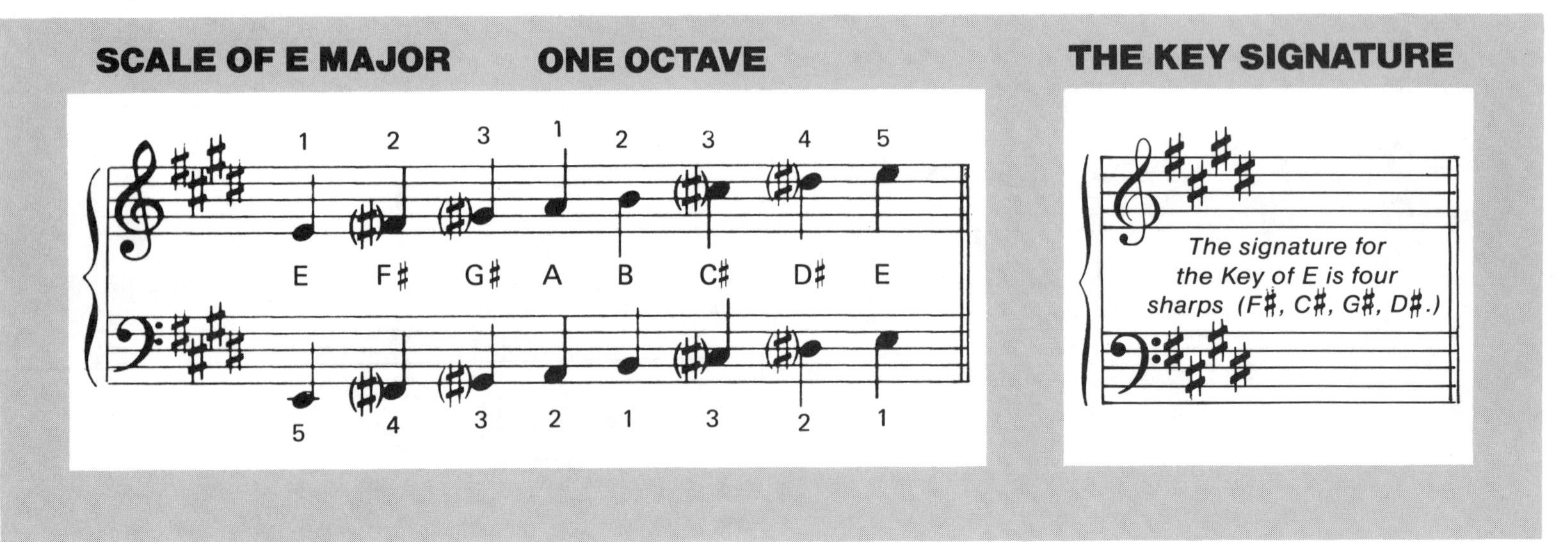

F CHORDS

All chords may be inverted. The Major Chord is shown with inversions to serve as an example.

F MAJOR (F) ROOT POSITION

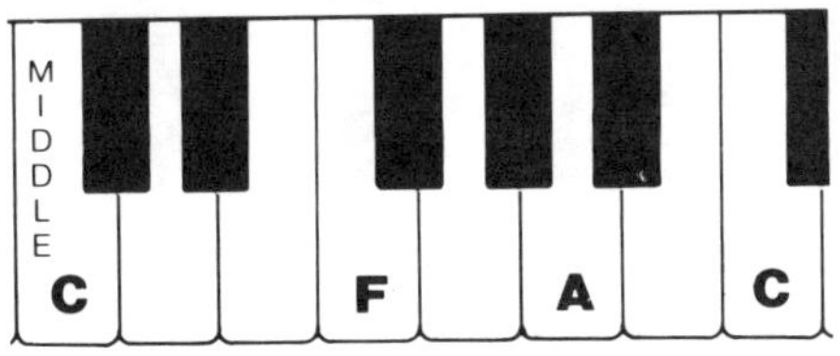

MIDDLE C — F — A — C

	F	A	C
R.H. →	1	3	5
L.H. →	5	3	1
BASS →	F or C		

1ST INVERSION ... OCTAVE LOWER

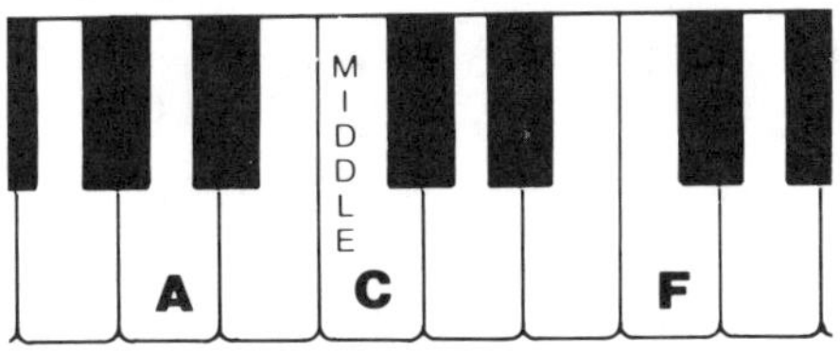

A — MIDDLE C — F

	A	C	F
R.H. →	1	2	5
L.H. →	5	3	1
BASS →	F or C		

2ND INVERSION . . . OCTAVE LOWER

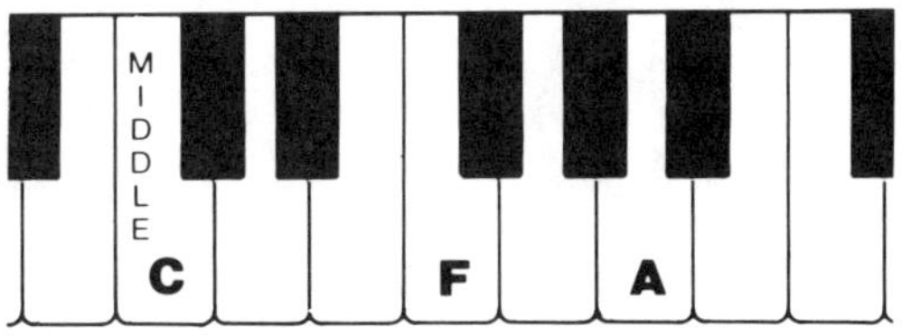

MIDDLE C — F — A

	C	F	A
R.H. →	1	3	5
L.H. →	5	2	1
BASS →	F or C		

F SIXTH (F6)

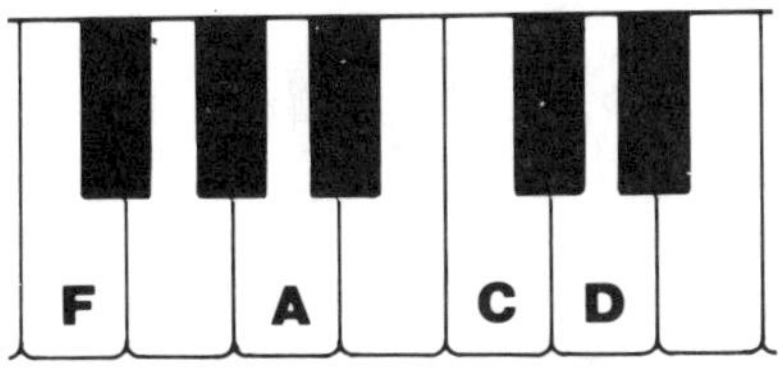

	F	A	C	D
R.H. →	1	2	4	5
L.H. →	5	3	2	1
BASS →	F or C			

F MAJOR SEVENTH (F maj 7)

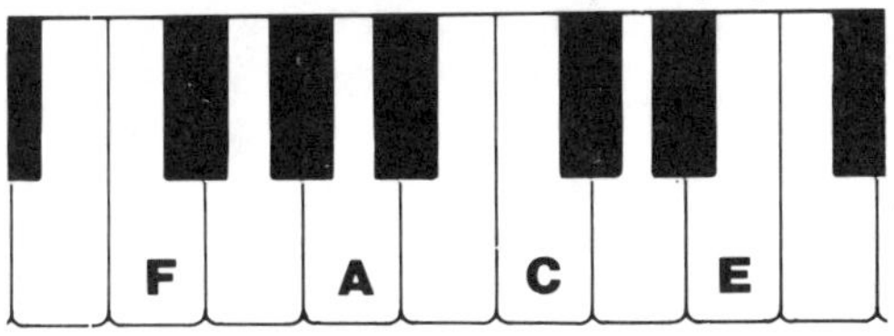

	F	A	C	E
R.H. →	1	2	3	5
L.H. →	5	3	2	1
BASS →	F or C			

F SEVENTH (F7)

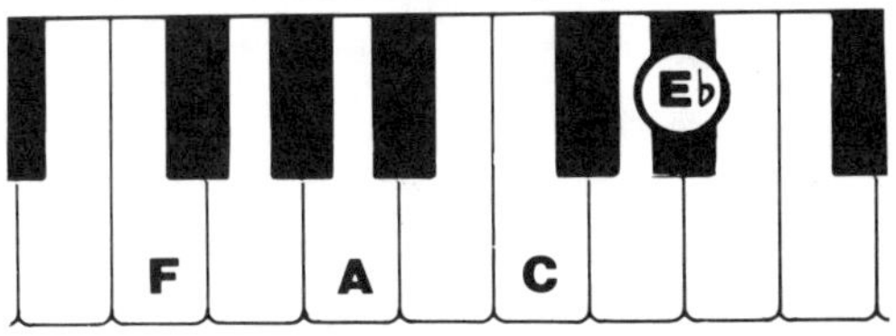

	F	A	C	E♭
R.H. →	1	2	3	5
L.H. →	5	3	2	1
BASS →	F or C			

F NINTH (F9)

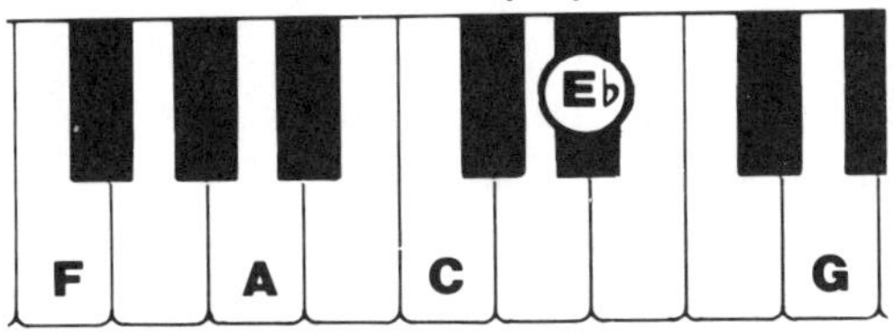

	F	A	C	E♭	G
R.H. →	1	2	3	4	5
L.H. →	5	4	3	2	1
BASS →	F or C				

F MAJOR NINTH (F maj 9)

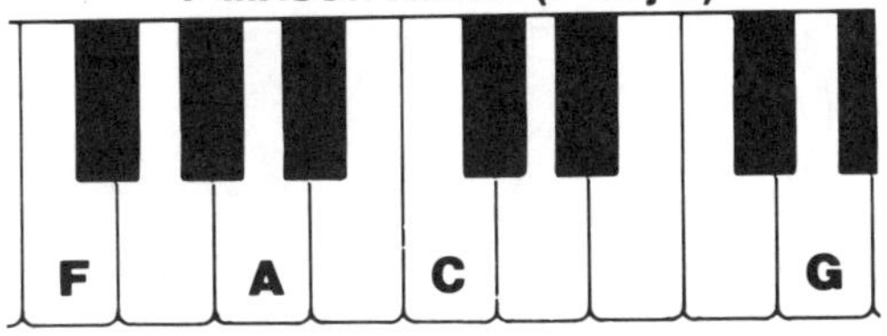

	F	A	C	G
R.H. →	1	2	3	5
L.H. →	5	3	2	1
BASS →	F or C			

F DIMINISHED (F°)

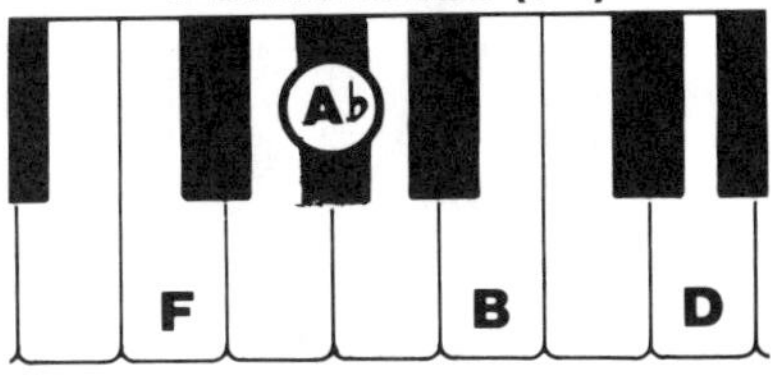

	F	A♭	B	D
R.H. →	1	2	3	5
L.H. →	5	3	2	1
BASS →	F			

F AUGMENTED (F+)

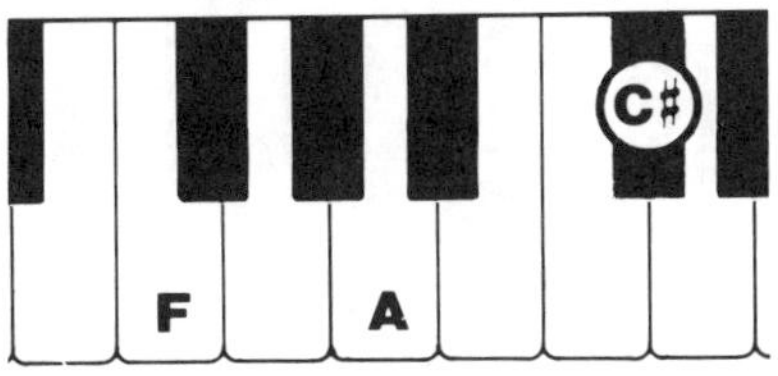

	F	A	C♯
R.H. →	1	2	4
L.H. →	5	3	1
BASS →	F		

F MINOR (Fm)

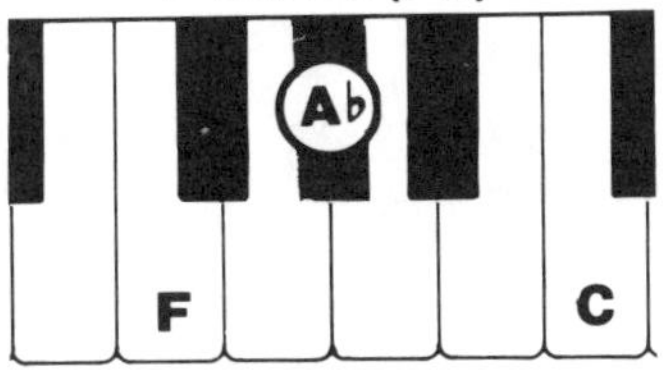

	F	A♭	C
R.H. →	1	3	5
L.H. →	5	3	1
BASS →	F or C		

F MINOR SIXTH (Fm6)

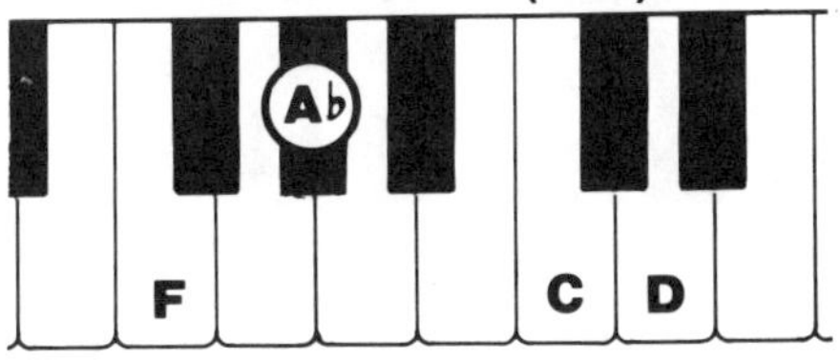

	F	A♭	C	D
R.H. →	1	2	4	5
L.H. →	5	3	2	1
BASS →	F or C			

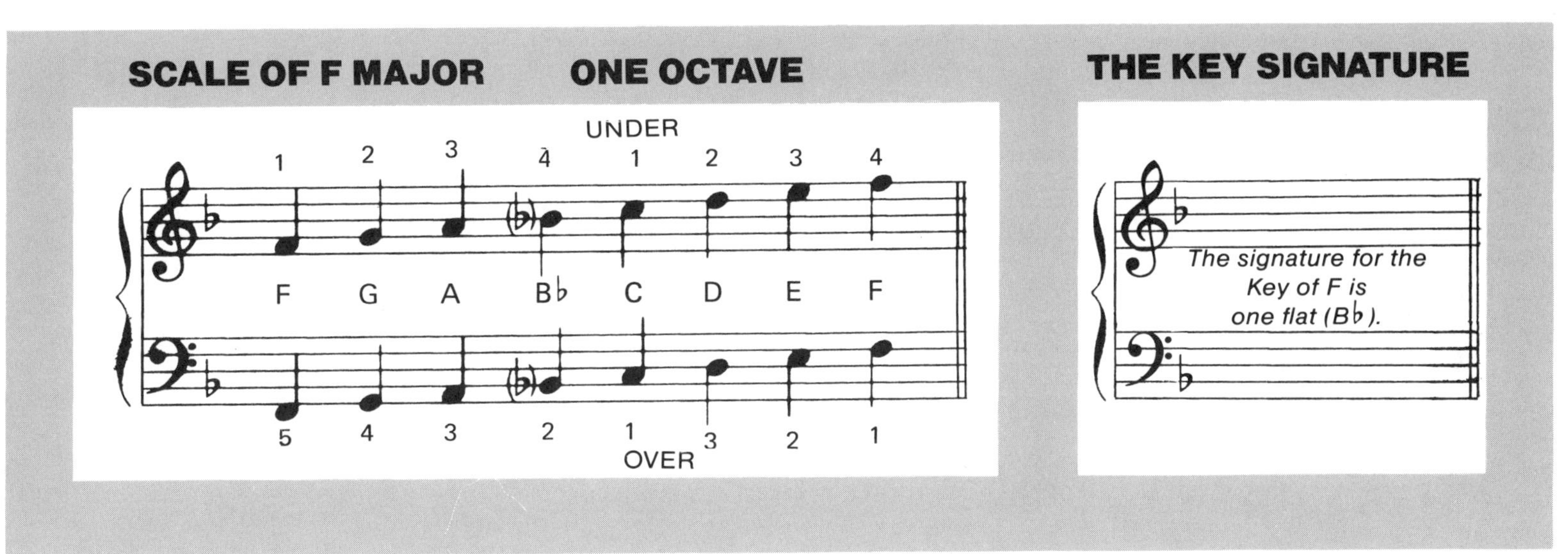

B♭ CHORDS

All chords mav be inverted The Major Chord is shown with inversions to serve as an example.

B♭ MAJOR (B♭) ROOT POSITION

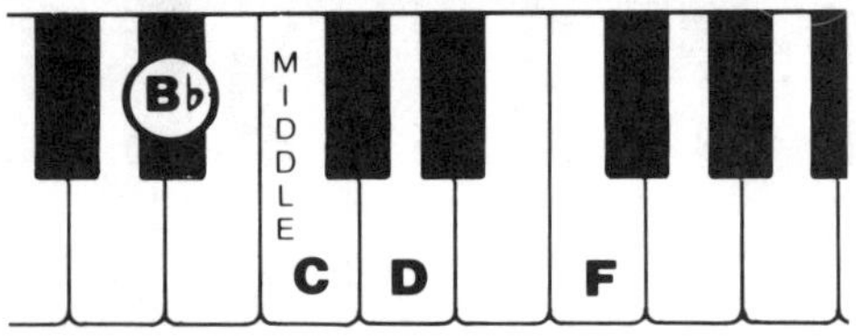

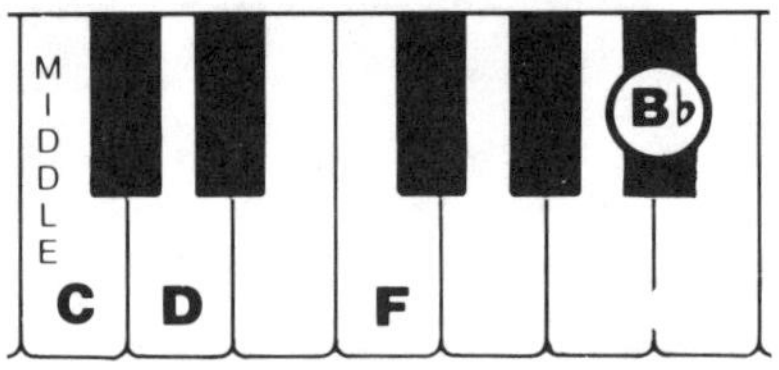

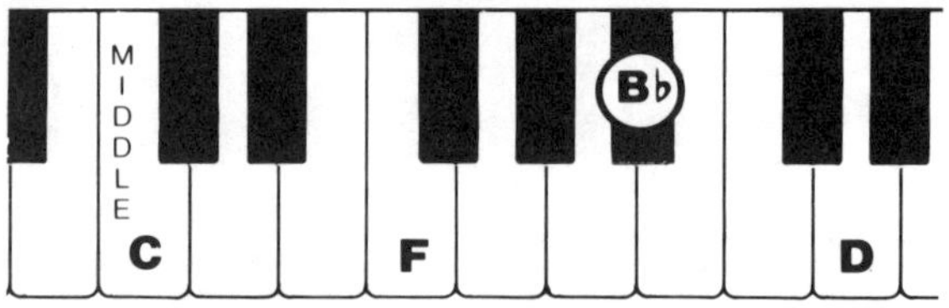

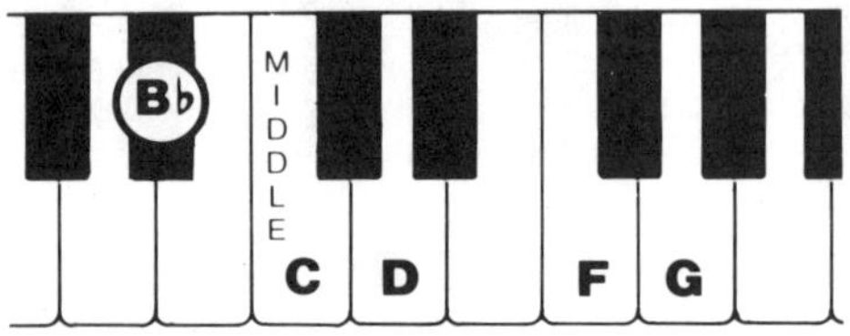

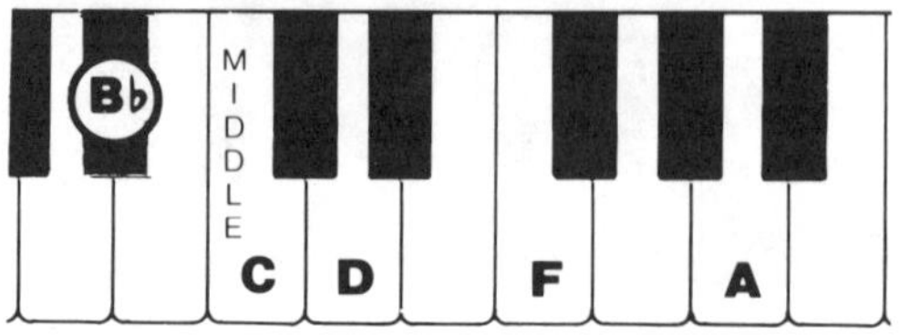

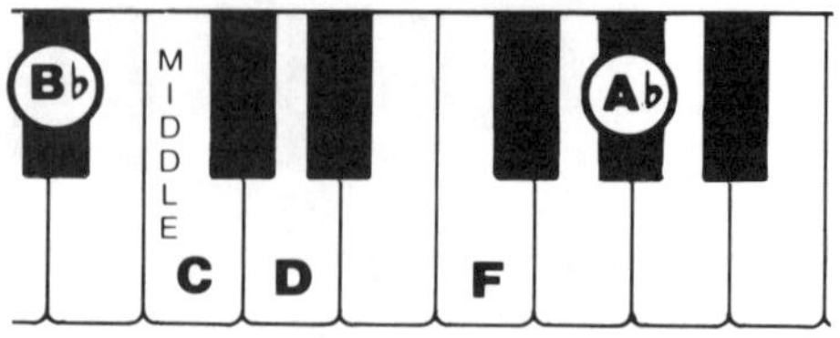

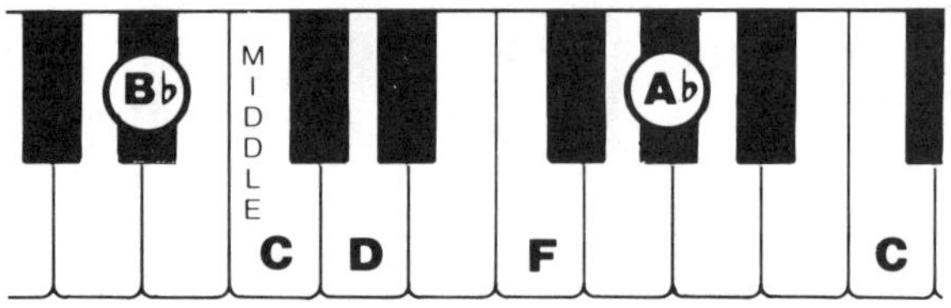

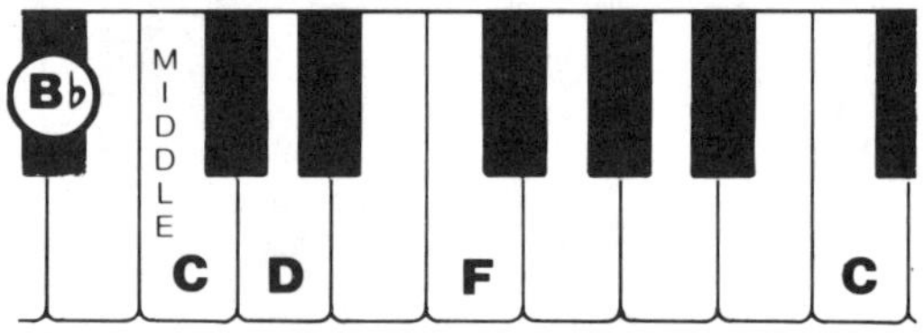

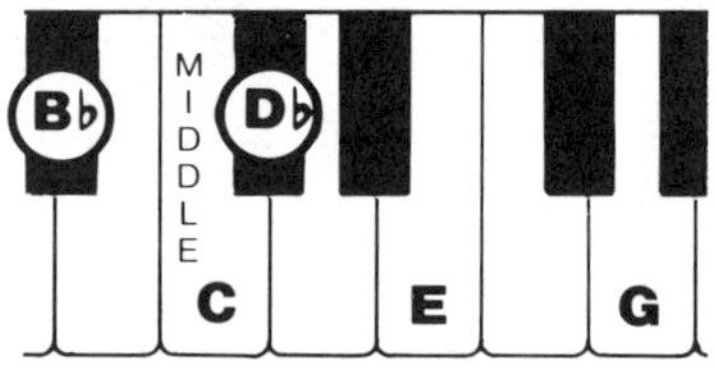

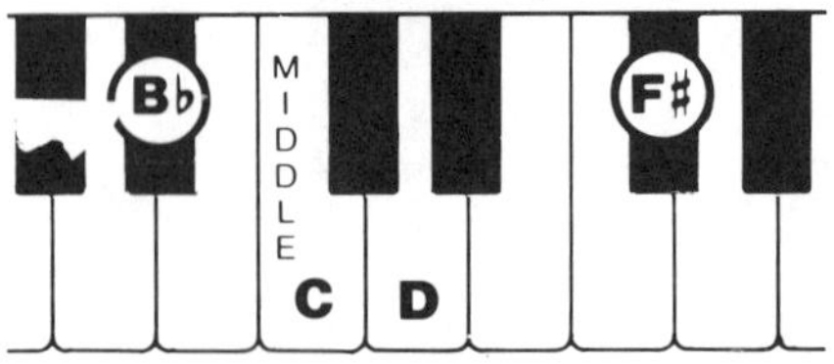

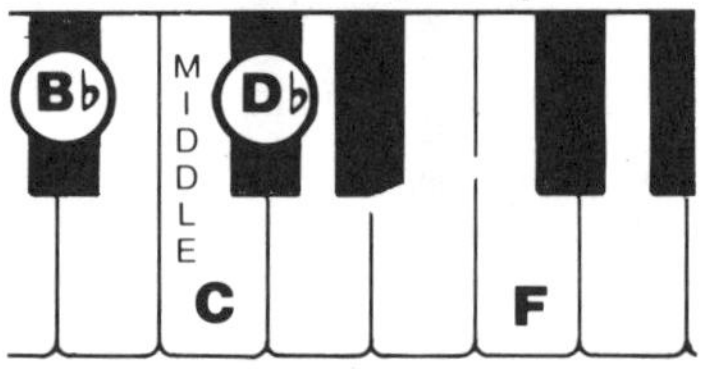

B♭
MIDDLE
C D F

R.H. → 1 3 5
L.H. → 5 3 1
BASS → B♭ or F

1ST INVERSION

MIDDLE
B♭
C D F

R.H. → 1 2 4
L.H. → 5 3 1
BASS → B♭ or F

2ND INVERSION

MIDDLE
B♭
C F D

R.H. → 1 3 5
L.H. → 5 3 1
BASS → B♭ or F

B♭ SIXTH (B♭6)

B♭
MIDDLE
C D F G

R.H. → 1 2 4 5
L.H. → 5 3 2 1
BASS → B♭ or F

B♭ MAJOR SEVENTH (B♭ maj 7)

B♭
MIDDLE
C D F A

R.H. → 1 2 3 5
L.H. → 5 3 2 1
BASS → B♭ or F

B♭ SEVENTH (B♭7)

B♭
MIDDLE
A♭
C D F

R.H. → 1 2 3 5
L.H. → 5 3 2 1
BASS → B♭ or F

B♭ NINTH (B♭9)

B♭
MIDDLE
A♭
C D F C

R.H. → 1 2 3 4 5
L.H. → 5 4 3 2 1
BASS → B♭ or F

B♭ MAJOR NINTH (B♭ maj 9)

B♭
MIDDLE
C D F C

R.H. → 1 2 3 5
L.H. → 5 3 2 1
BASS → B♭ or F

B♭ DIMINISHED (B♭°)

B♭
MIDDLE
D♭
C E G

R.H. → 1 2 3 5
L.H. → 5 3 2 1
BASS → B♭

B♭ AUGMENTED (B♭+)

B♭
MIDDLE
F♯
C D

R.H. → 1 3 5
L.H. → 5 3 1
BASS → B♭

B♭ MINOR (B♭m)

B♭
MIDDLE
D♭
C F

R.H. → 1 3 5
L.H. → 5 3 1
BASS → B♭ or F

B♭ MINOR SIXTH (B♭m6)

B♭
MIDDLE
D♭
C F G

R.H. → 1 2 4 5
L.H. → 5 3 2 1
BASS → B♭ or F

SCALE OF B♭ MAJOR ONE OCTAVE

4 1 2 3 1 2 3 4
B♭ C D E♭ F G A B♭
3 2 1 4 3 2 1 3

THE KEY SIGNATURE

The signature for
the Key of B♭
is two flats (B♭ and E♭.)

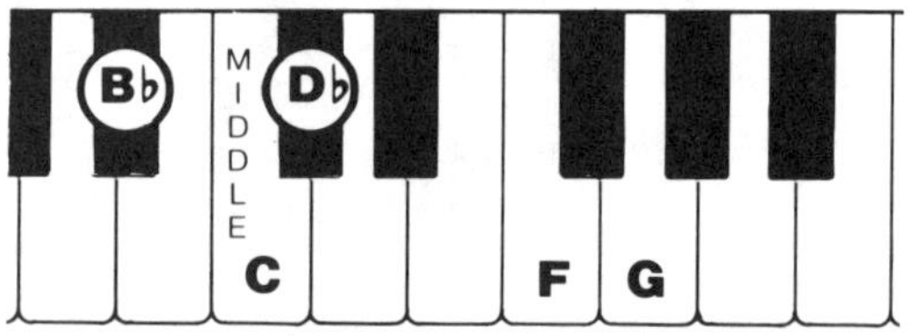

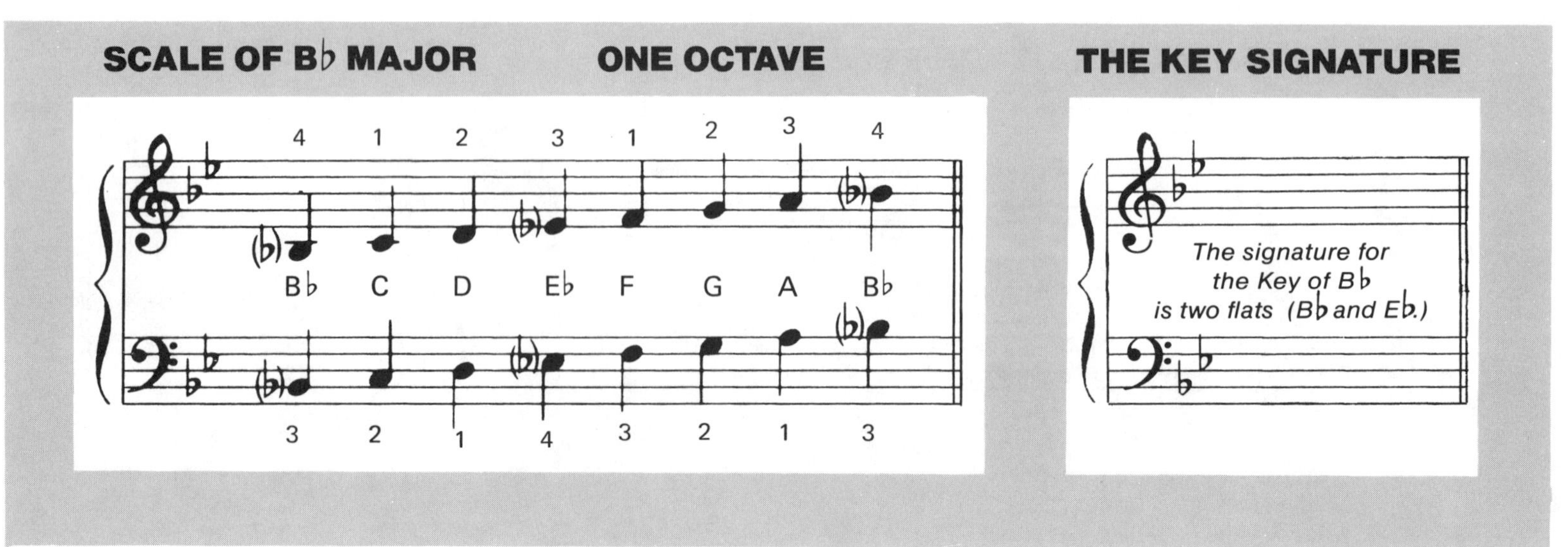

E♭ CHORDS

All chords may be inverted. The Major Chord is shown with inversions to serve as an example.

E♭ MAJOR (E♭) ROOT POSITION

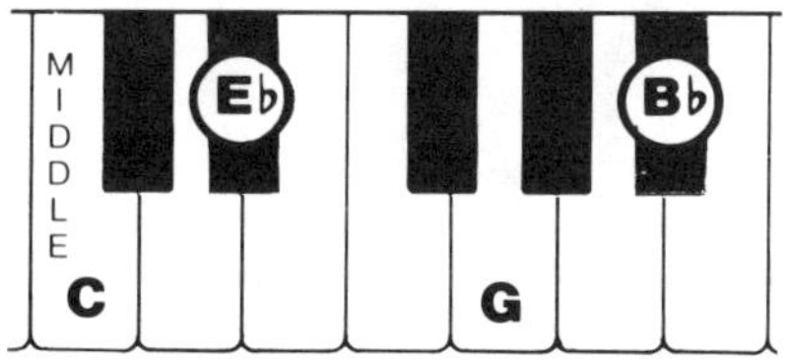

Keys: MIDDLE C, E♭, G, B♭

R.H. →	1	3	5
L.H. →	5	3	1
BASS →	E♭ or B♭		

1ST INVERSION

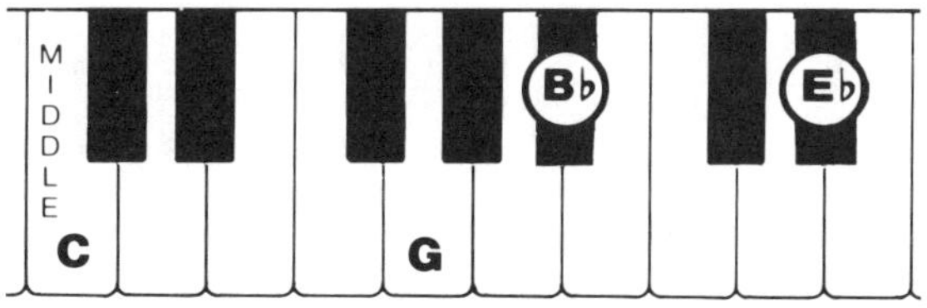

Keys: MIDDLE C, G, B♭, E♭

R.H. →	1	2	5
L.H. →	5	3	1
BASS →	E♭ or B♭		

2ND INVERSION . . . OCTAVE LOWER

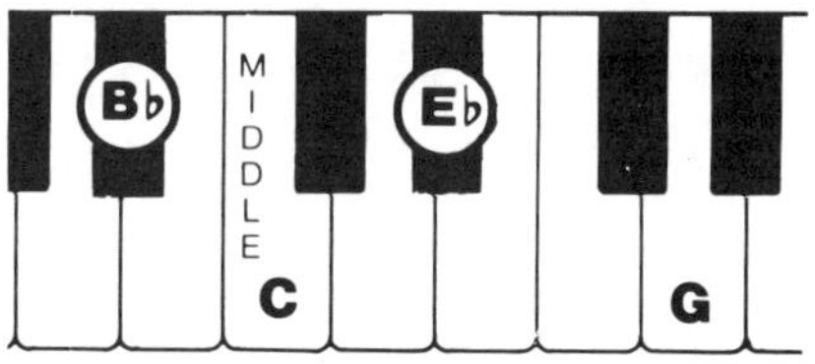

Keys: B♭, MIDDLE C, E♭, G

R.H. →	1	3	5
L.H. →	5	3	1
BASS →	E♭ or B♭		

E♭ SIXTH (E♭6)

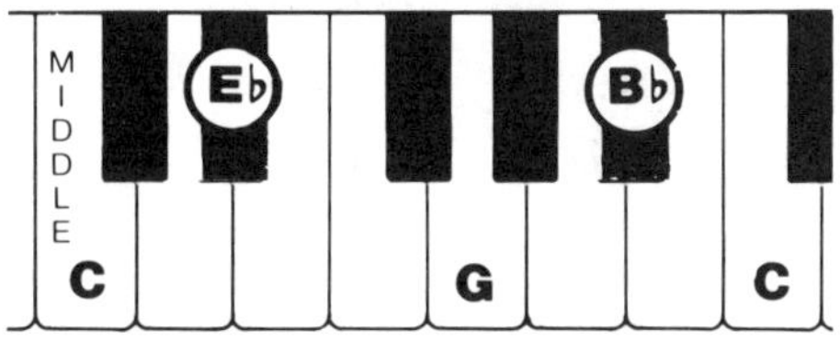

Keys: MIDDLE C, E♭, G, B♭, C

R.H. →	1	2	4	5
L.H. →	5	3	2	1
BASS →	E♭ or B♭			

E♭ MAJOR SEVENTH (E♭ maj 7)

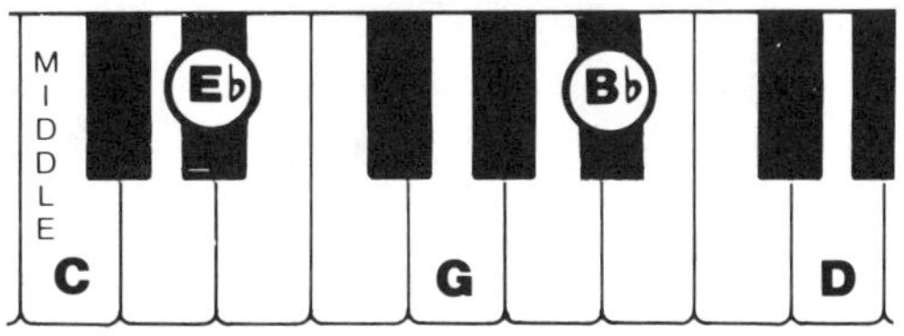

Keys: MIDDLE C, E♭, G, B♭, D

R.H. →	1	2	3	5
L.H. →	5	3	2	1
BASS →	E♭ or B♭			

E♭ SEVENTH (E♭7)

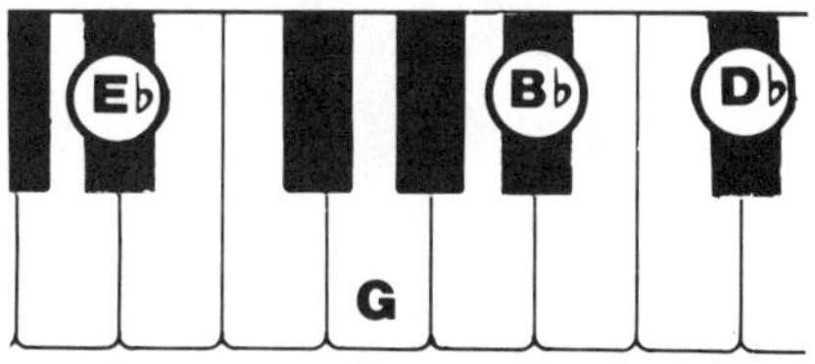

Keys: E♭, G, B♭, D♭

R.H. →	1	2	3	5
L.H. →	5	3	2	1
BASS →	E♭ or B♭			

E♭ NINTH (E♭9)

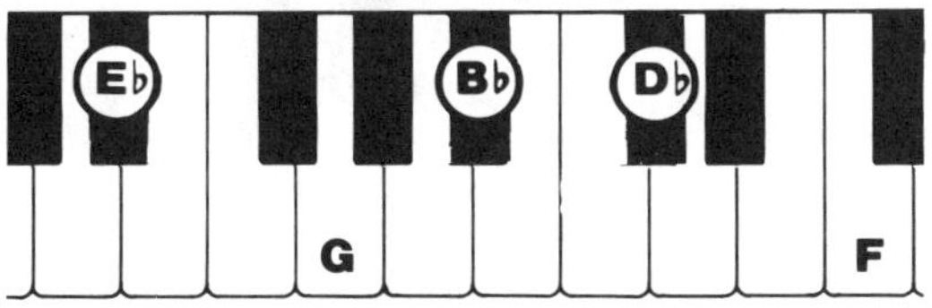

Keys: E♭, G, B♭, D♭, F

R.H. →	1	2	3	4	5
L.H. →	5	4	3	2	1
BASS →	E♭ or B♭				

E♭ MAJOR NINTH (E♭ maj 9)

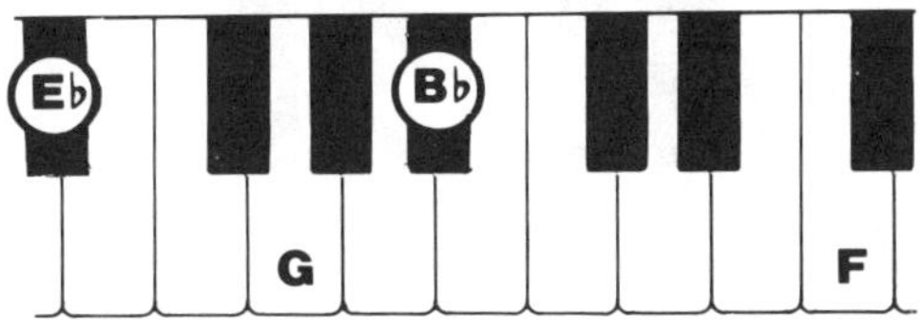

Keys: E♭, G, B♭, F

R.H. →	1	2	3	5
L.H. →	5	3	2	1
BASS →	E♭ or B♭			

E♭ DIMINISHED (E♭°)

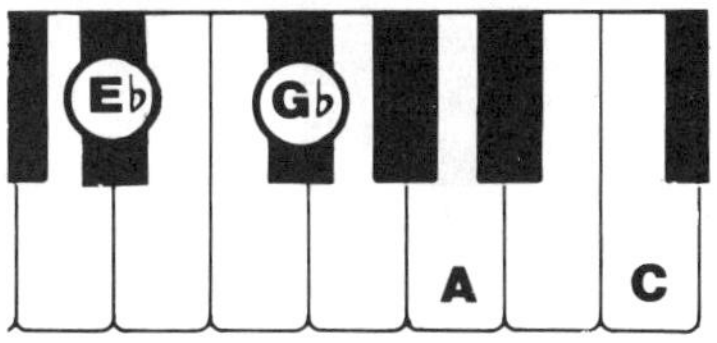

Keys: E♭, G♭, A, C

R.H. →	1	2	3	5
L.H. →	5	3	2	1
BASS →	E♭			

E♭ AUGMENTED (E♭+)

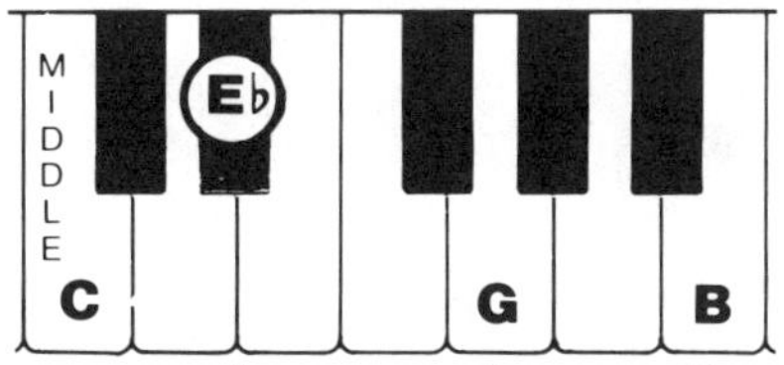

Keys: MIDDLE C, E♭, G, B

R.H. →	1	3	5
L.H. →	5	3	1
BASS →	E♭		

E♭ MINOR (E♭m)

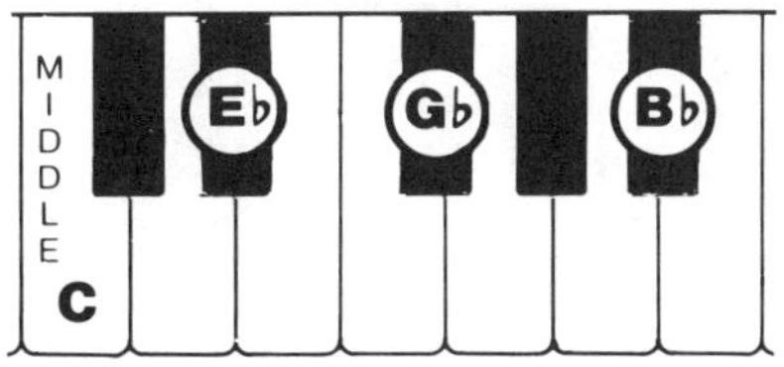

Keys: MIDDLE C, E♭, G♭, B♭

R.H. →	1	3	5
L.H. →	5	3	1
BASS →	E♭ or B♭		

E♭ MINOR SIXTH (E♭m6)

Keys: MIDDLE C, E♭, G♭, B♭, C

R.H. →	1	2	4	5
L.H. →	5	3	2	1
BASS →	E♭ or B♭			

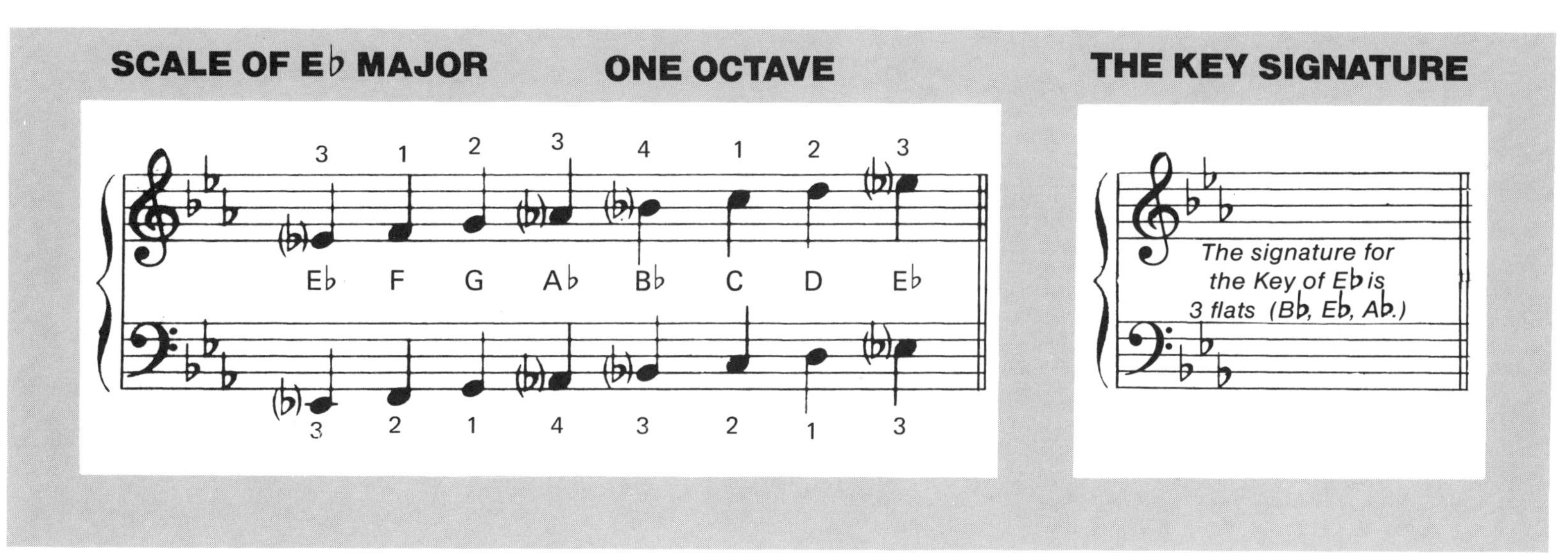

A♭ CHORDS

All chords may be inverted. The Major Chord is shown with inversions to serve as an example.

A♭ MAJOR (A♭) ROOT POSITION

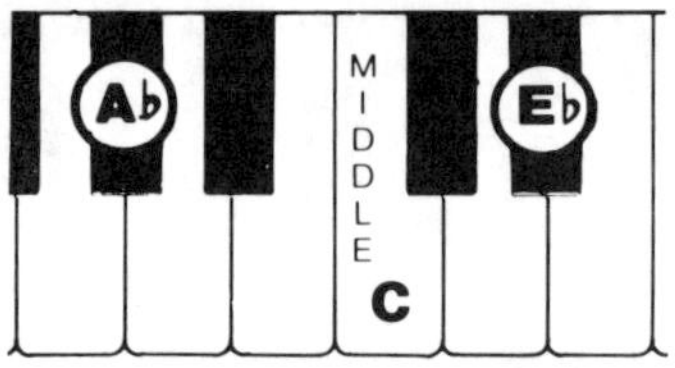

A♭
MIDDLE
C
E♭

R.H. →	1	3	5
L.H. →	5	3	1
BASS →	A♭ or E♭		

1ST INVERSION

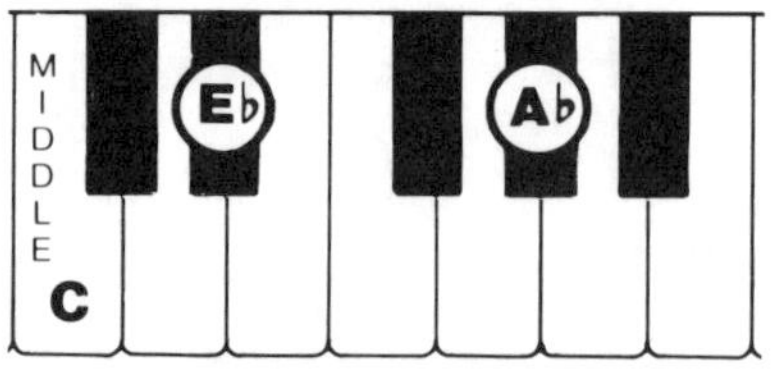

MIDDLE
C
E♭
A♭

R.H. →	1	2	5
L.H. →	5	3	1
BASS →	A♭ or E♭		

2ND INVERSION

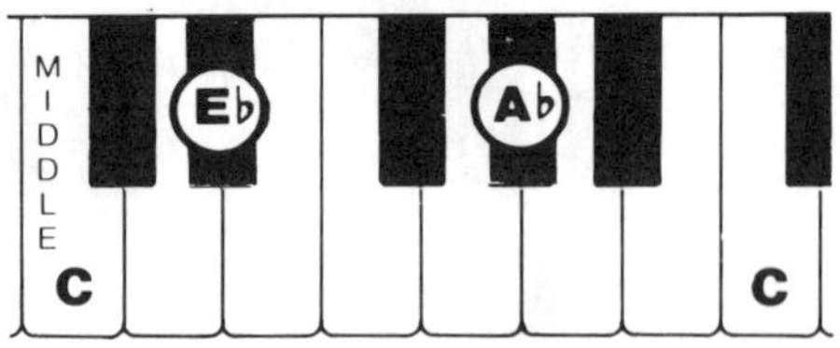

MIDDLE
C
E♭
A♭
C

R.H. →	1	3	5
L.H. →	5	3	1
BASS →	A♭ or E♭		

A♭ SIXTH (A♭6)

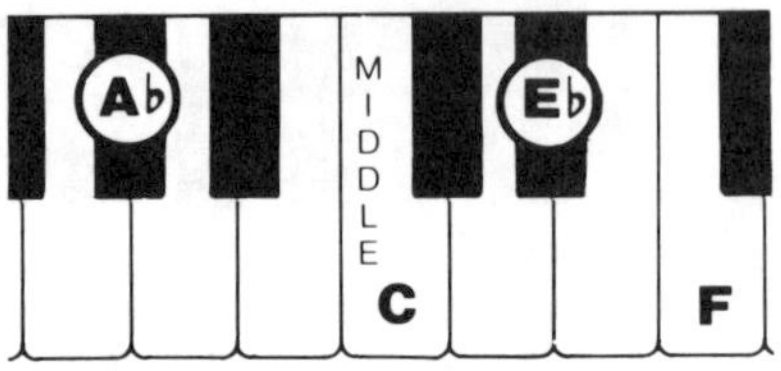

A♭
MIDDLE
C
E♭
F

R.H. →	1	2	4	5
L.H. →	5	3	2	1
BASS →	A♭ or E♭			

A♭ MAJOR SEVENTH (A♭maj 7)

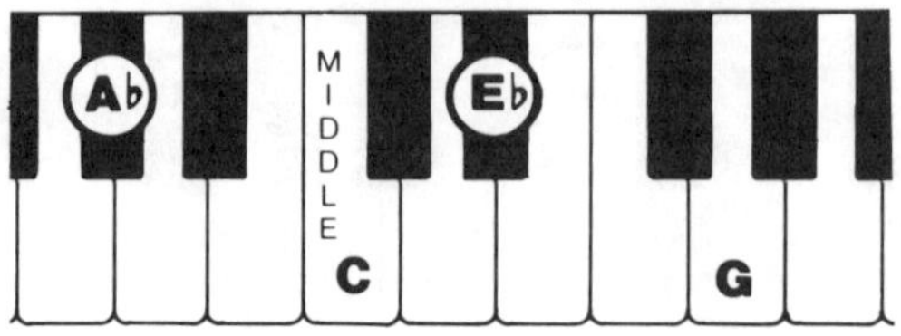

A♭
MIDDLE
C
E♭
G

R.H. →	1	2	3	5
L.H. →	5	3	2	1
BASS →	A♭ or E♭			

A♭ SEVENTH (A♭7)

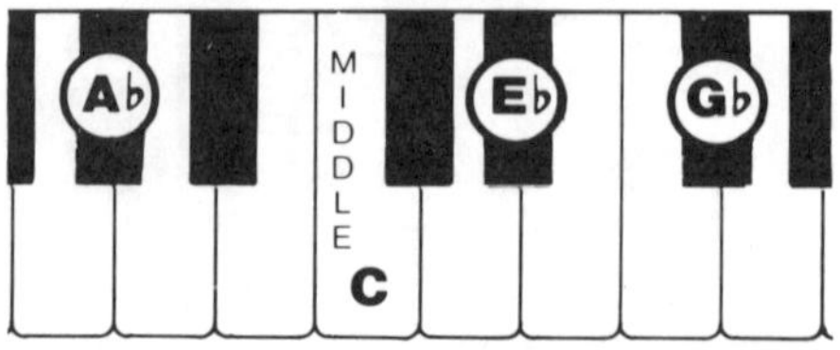

A♭
MIDDLE
C
E♭
G♭

R.H. →	1	2	3	5
L.H. →	5	3	2	1
BASS →	A♭ or E♭			

A♭ NINTH (A♭9)

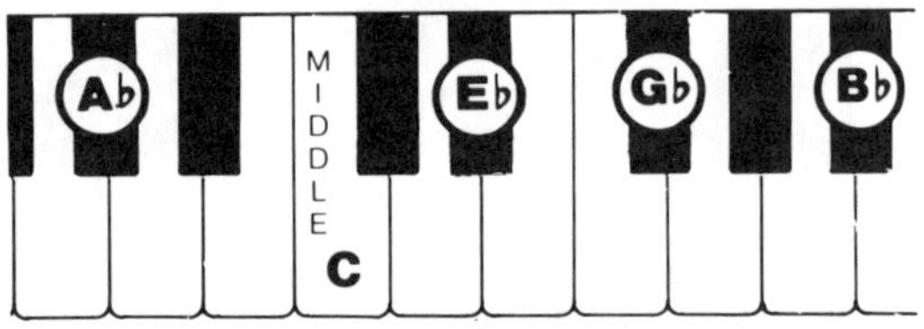

A♭
MIDDLE
C
E♭
G♭
B♭

R.H. →	1	2	3	4	5
L.H. →	5	4	3	2	1
BASS →	A♭ or E♭				

A♭ MAJOR NINTH (A♭maj 9)

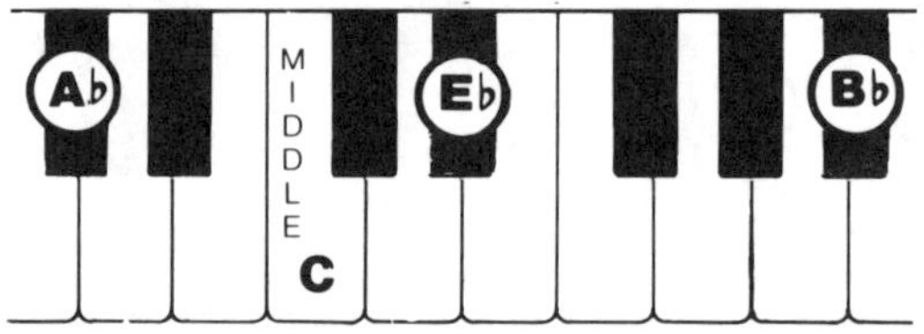

A♭
MIDDLE
C
E♭
B♭

R.H. →	1	2	3	5
L.H. →	5	3	2	1
BASS →	A♭ or E♭			

A♭ DIMINISHED (A♭°)

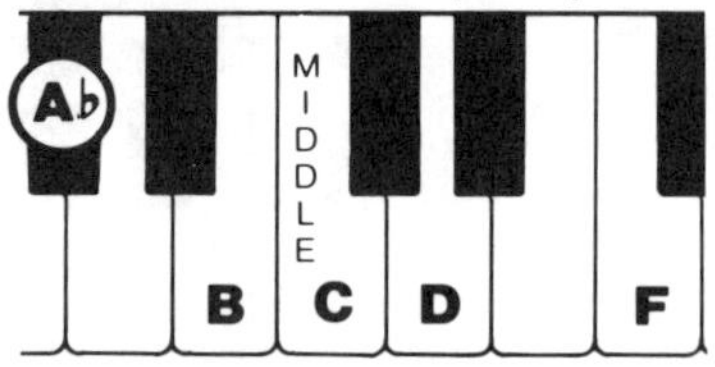

A♭
B
MIDDLE
C
D
F

R.H. →	1	2	3	5
L.H. →	5	3	2	1
BASS →	A♭			

A♭ AUGMENTED (A♭+)

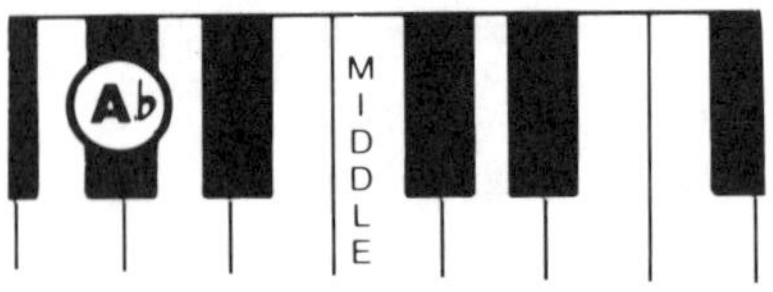

A♭
MIDDLE

R.H. –			
L.H. →	5	3	1
BASS →	A♭		

A♭ MINOR (A♭m)

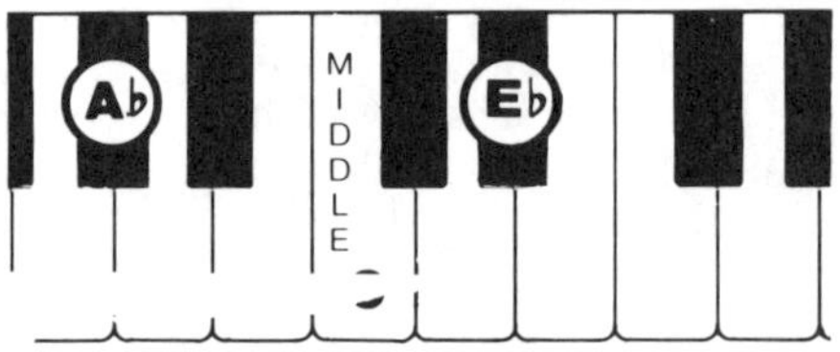

A♭
MIDDLE
E♭

R.H.	1	3	5
L.H.	5	3	1
BASS →	A♭ or E♭		

A♭ MINOR SIXTH (A♭m6)

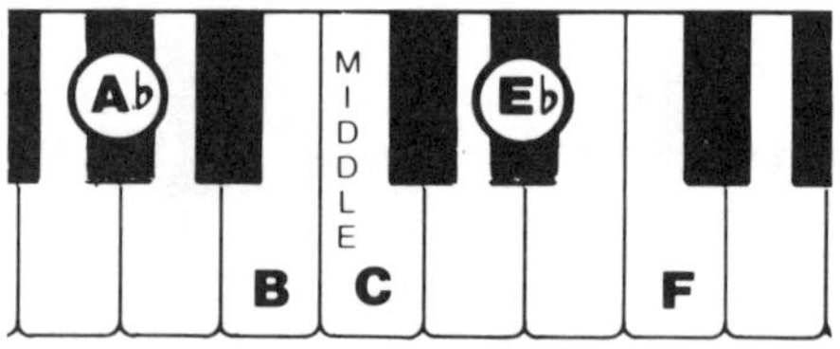

A♭
B
MIDDLE
C
E♭
F

R.H.	1	2	4	5
L.H.	5	3	2	1
BASS →	A♭ or E♭			

SCALE OF A♭ MAJOR ONE OCTAVE

3 4 1 2 3 1 2 3
A♭ B♭ C D♭ E♭ F G A♭
3 2 1 4 3 2 1 3

THE KEY SIGNATURE

The signature for the Key of A♭ is 4 flats (B♭, E♭, A♭, D♭.)

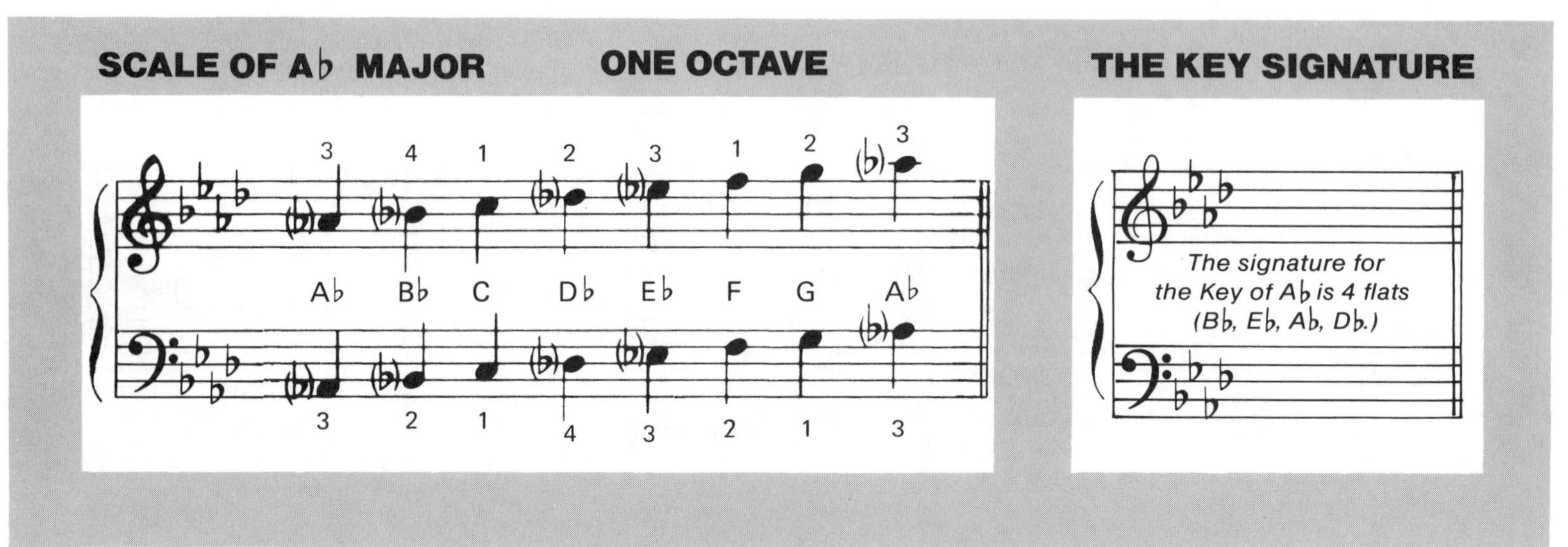

D♭ CHORDS

All chords may be inverted. The Major Chord is shown with inversions to serve as an example.

D♭ MAJOR CHORD (D♭) ROOT POSITION
Keys: D♭ A♭ (Middle C, F)

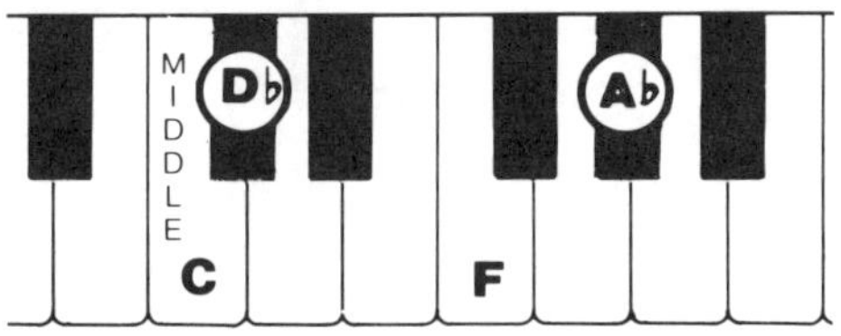

R.H. →	1	3	5
L.H. →	5	3	1
BASS →	D♭ or A♭		

1ST INVERSION
Keys: A♭ D♭ (Middle C, F)

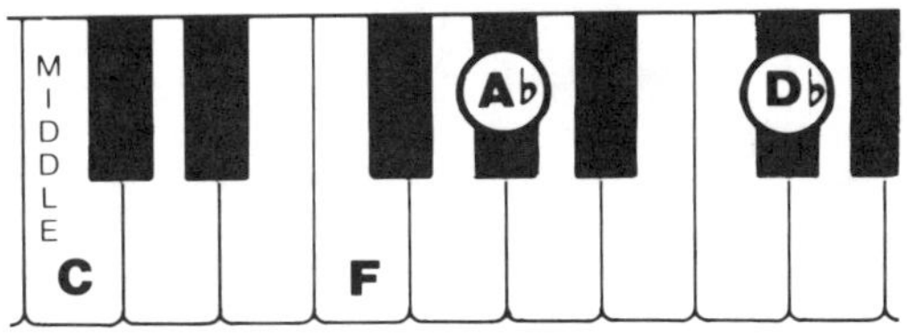

R.H. →	1	2	5
L.H. →	5	3	1
BASS →	D♭ or A♭		

2ND INVERSION ... OCTAVE LOWER
Keys: A♭ D♭ (Middle C, F)

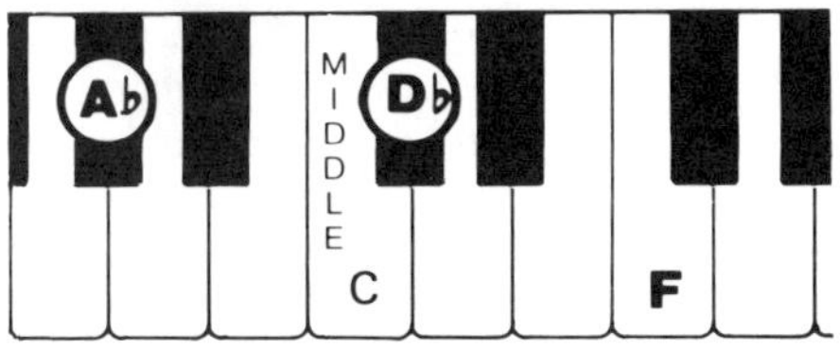

R.H. →	1	3	5
L.H. →	5	3	1
BASS →	D♭ or A♭		

D♭ SIXTH (D♭6)
Keys: D♭ A♭ B♭ (Middle C, F)

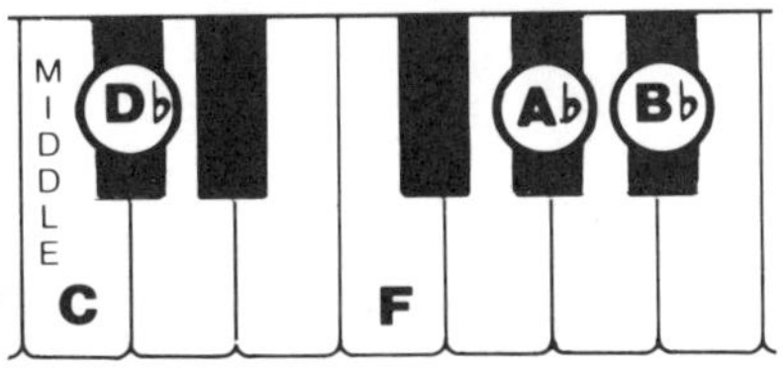

R.H. →	1	2	4	5
L.H. →	5	3	2	1
BASS →	D♭ or A♭			

D♭ MAJOR SEVENTH (D♭ maj 7)
Keys: D♭ A♭ (Middle C, F, C)

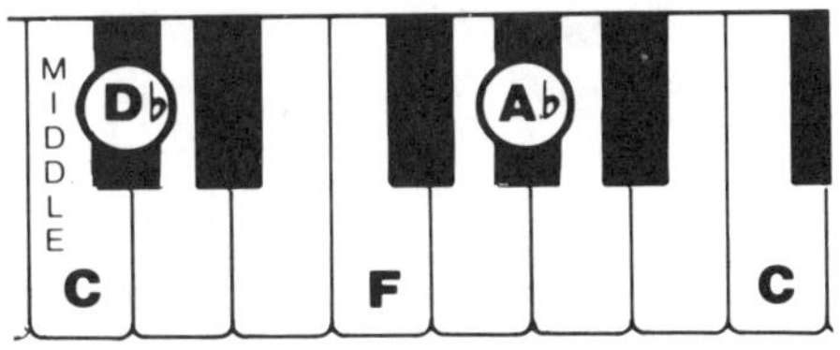

R.H. →	1	2	3	5
L.H. →	5	3	2	1
BASS →	D♭ or A♭			

D♭ SEVENTH (D♭7)
Keys: D♭ A♭ (Middle C, F, B)

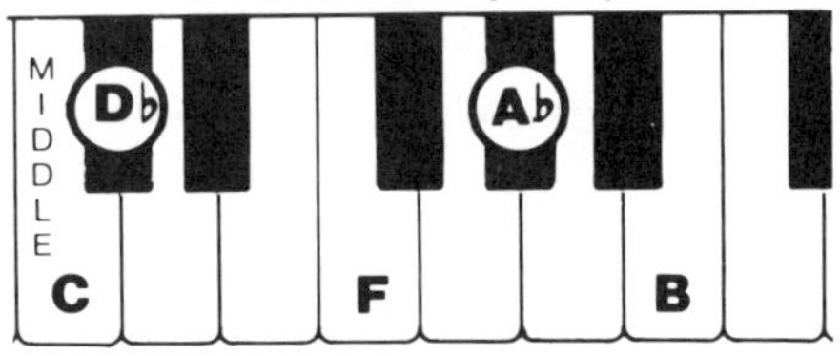

R.H. →	1	2	3	5
L.H. →	5	3	2	1
BASS →	D♭ or A♭			

D♭ NINTH (D♭9)
Keys: D♭ A♭ E♭ (Middle C, F, B)

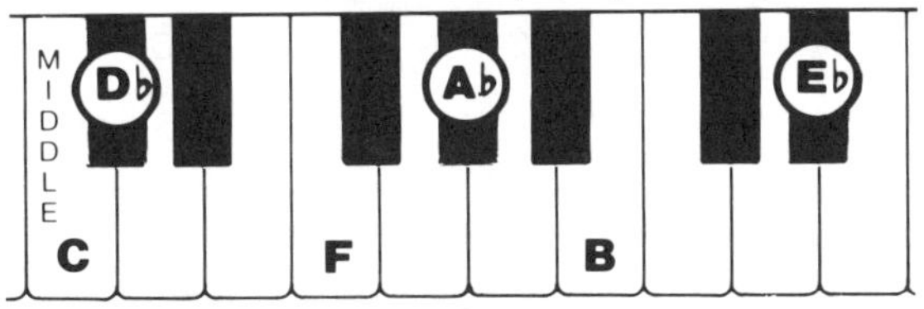

R.H. →	1	2	3	4	5
L.H. →	5	4	3	2	1
BASS →	D♭ or A♭				

D♭ MAJOR NINTH (D♭ maj 9)
Keys: D♭ A♭ E♭ (Middle C, F)

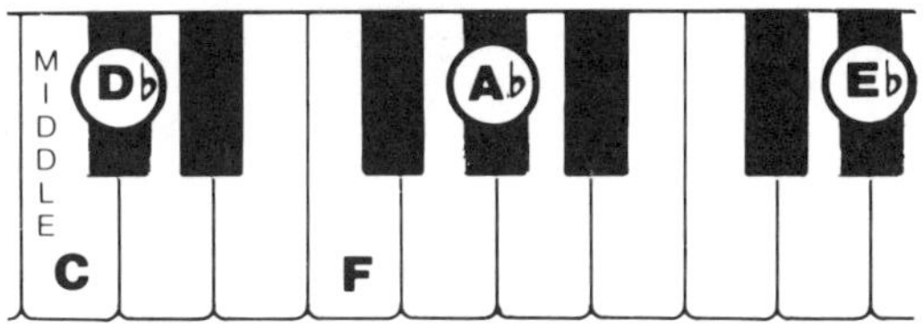

R.H. →	1	2	3	5
L.H. →	5	3	2	1
BASS →	D♭ or A♭			

D♭ DIMINISHED (D♭°)
Keys: D♭ B♭ (Middle C, E, G)

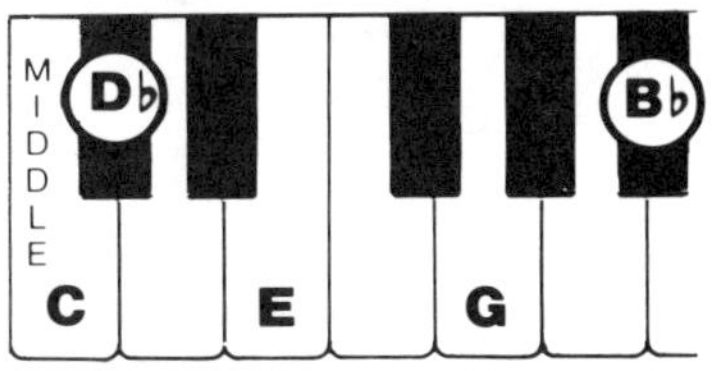

R.H. →	1	2	3	5
L.H. →	5	3	2	1
BASS →	D♭			

D♭ AUGMENTED (D♭+)
Keys: D♭ (Middle C, F, A)

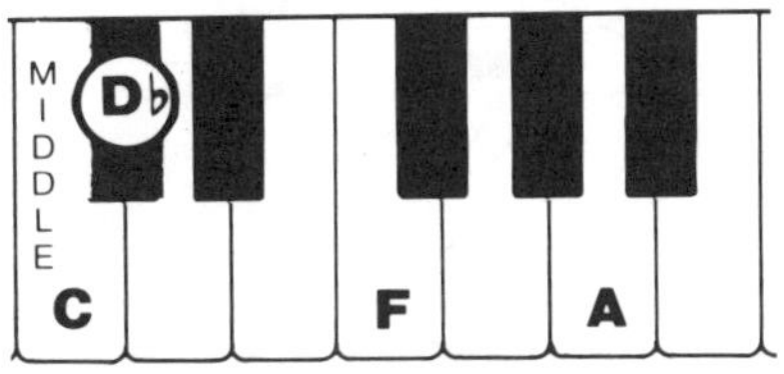

R.H. →	1	3	5
L.H. →	5	3	1
BASS →	D♭		

D♭ MINOR (D♭m)
Keys: D♭ A♭ (Middle C, E)

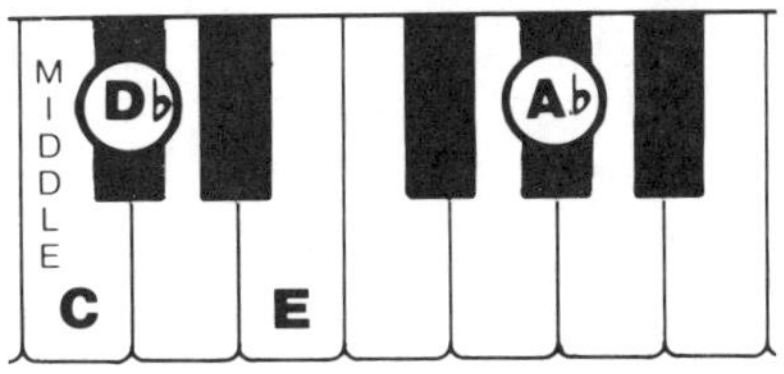

R.H. →	1	3	5
L.H. →	5	3	1
BASS →	D♭ or A♭		

D♭ MINOR SIXTH (D♭m6)
Keys: D♭ A♭ B♭ (Middle C, E)

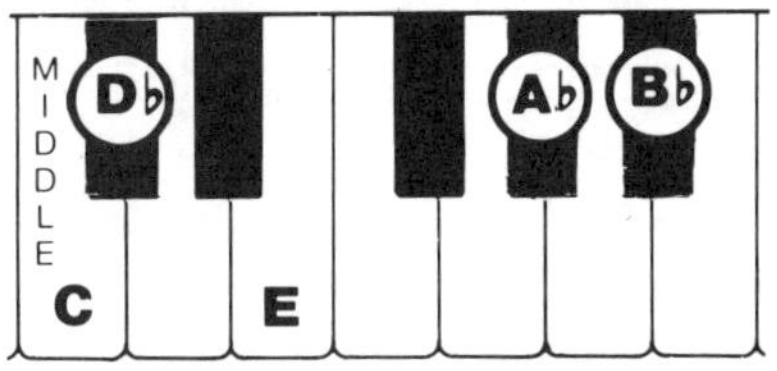

R.H. →	1	2	4	5
L.H. →	5	3	2	1
BASS →	D♭ or A♭			

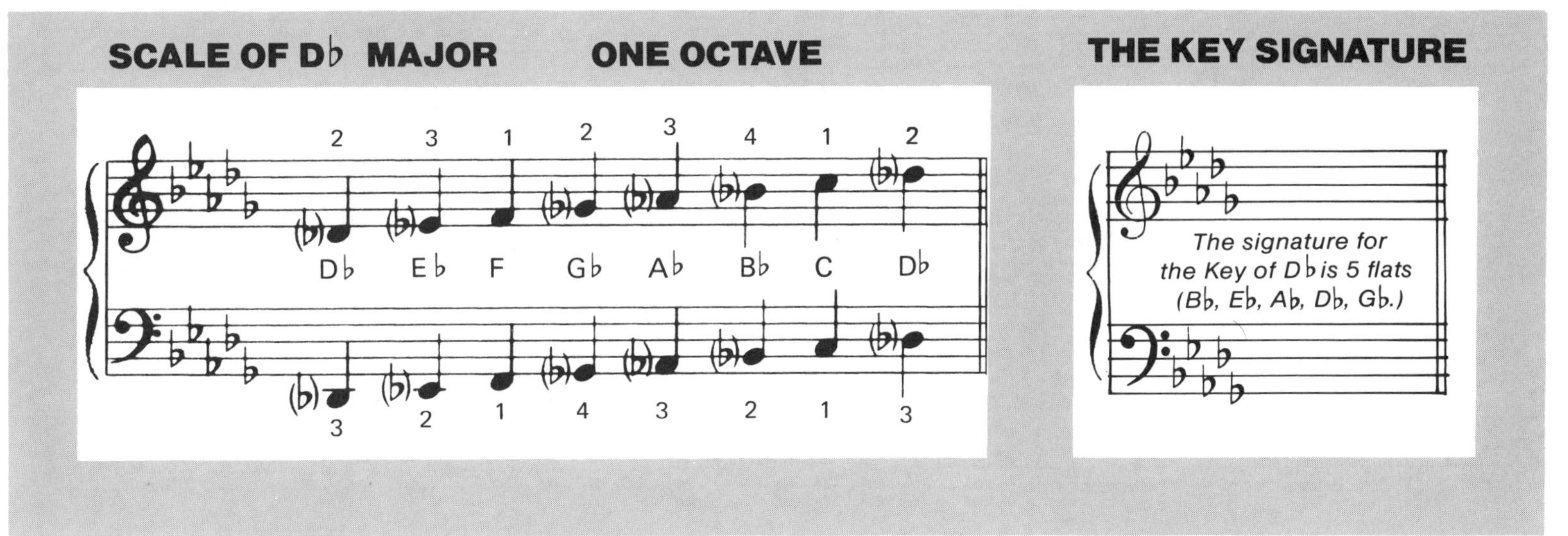

DOTTED EIGHTH NOTES AND SIXTEENTH NOTES

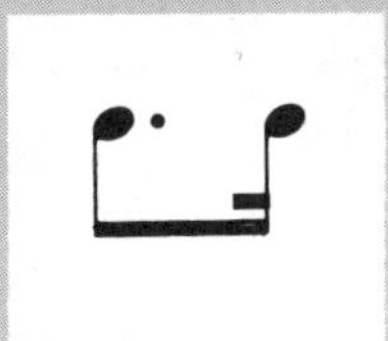

In 3/4, or 4/4 time, the combination of a dotted eighth note and a sixteenth note will total one full count. The dotted eighth receives 3/4 of a count and the sixteenth receives 1/4 of a count. This style is played with a rhythmic bounce.

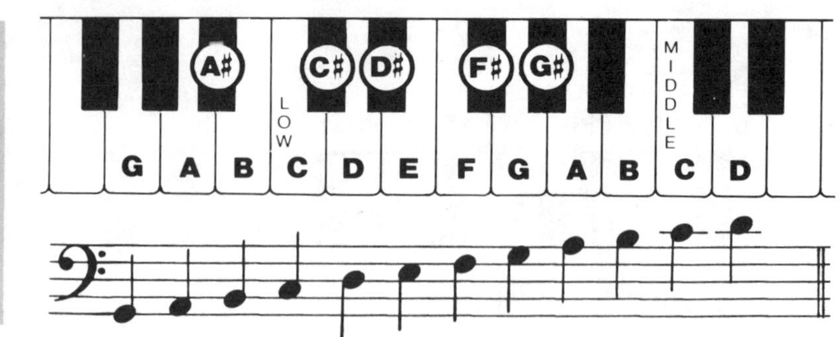

BASS PATTERNS

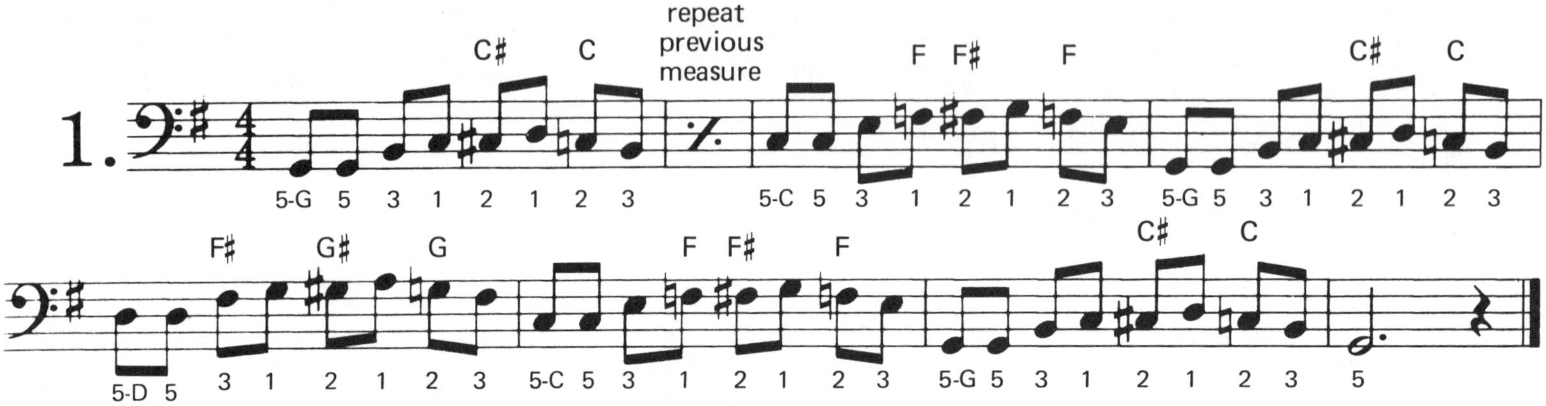

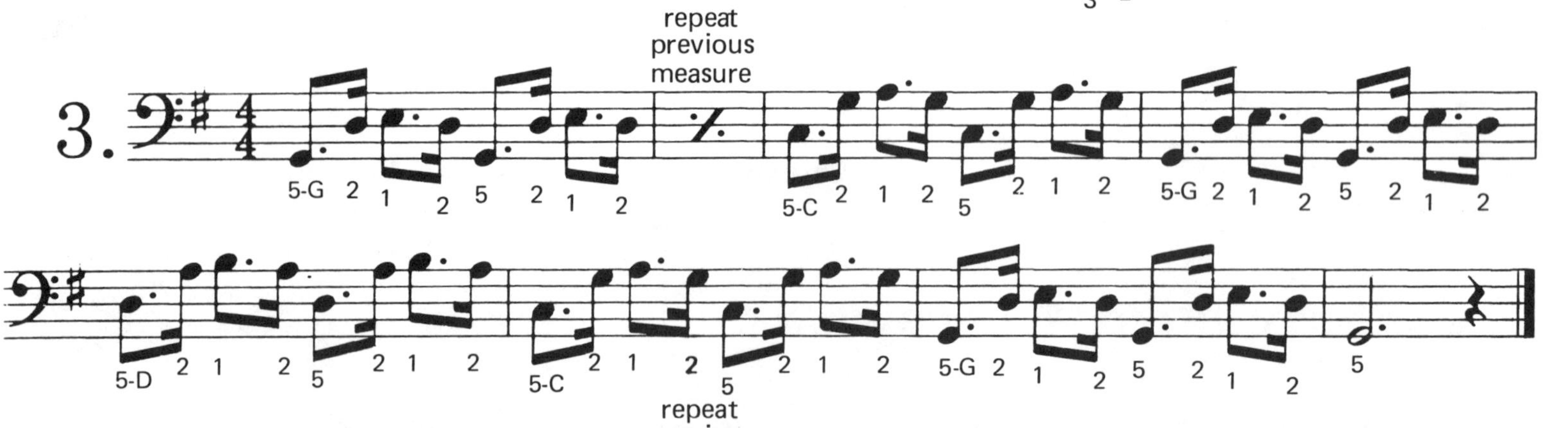

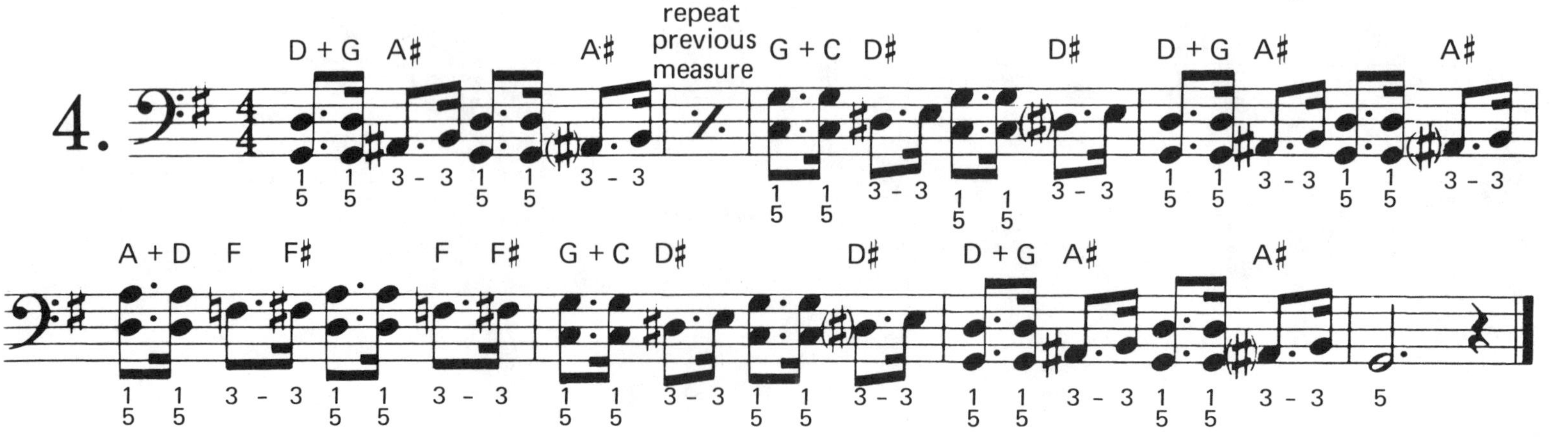

1.
C♯ C
repeat previous measure
F F♯ F
C♯ C
5-G 5 3 1 2 1 2 3
5-C 5 3 1 2 1 2 3
5-G 5 3 1 2 1 2 3

F♯ G♯ G
F F♯ F
C♯ C
5-D 5 3 1 2 1 2 3
5-C 5 3 1 2 1 2 3
5-G 5 3 1 2 1 2 3
5

2.
repeat previous measure
5-G 1 3 2 3 2
5-C 1 3 2 3 2
5-G 1 3 2 3 2

5-D 1 3 2 3 2
5-C 1 3 2 3 2
5-G 1 3 2 3 2
5

3.
repeat previous measure
5-G 2 1 2 5 2 1 2
5-C 2 1 2 5 2 1 2
5-G 2 1 2 5 2 1 2

5-D 2 1 2 5 2 1 2
5-C 2 1 2 5 2 1 2
5-G 2 1 2 5 2 1 2
5

4.
D + G A♯ A♯
repeat previous measure
G + C D♯ D♯
D + G A♯ A♯
1/5 1/5 3 - 3 1/5 1/5 3 - 3
1/5 1/5 3 - 3 1/5 1/5 3 - 3
1/5 1/5 3 - 3 1/5 1/5 3 - 3

A + D F F♯ F F♯
G + C D♯ D♯
D + G A♯ A♯
1/5 1/5 3 - 3 1/5 1/5 3 - 3
1/5 1/5 3 - 3 1/5 1/5 3 - 3
1/5 1/5 3 - 3 1/5 1/5 3 - 3
5